SEVEN
SIGNATORIES

SEVEN
SIGNATORIES

Tracing the Family Histories of the Men
Who Signed the Proclamation

Paul Gorry

MERRION
PRESS

Published in 2016 by
Merrion Press
10 George's Street
Newbridge
Co. Kildare
Ireland
www.merrionpress.ie

© 2016 Paul Gorry

ISBN: 978-1-78537-099-1 (paperback)
ISBN: 978-1-78537-100-4 (Kindle)
ISBN: 978-1-78537-100-4 (Epub)

British Library Cataloguing in Publication Data
An entry can be found on request

Library of Congress Cataloging in Publication Data
An entry can be found on request

Design by www.jminfotechindia.com
Typeset in Adobe Garamond Pro 11/15 pt
Cover design by www.phoenix-graphicdesign.com

Kildare County Council
Comhairle Contae Chill Dara

Printed in Ireland by SPRINT-print Ltd

CONTENTS

PICTURE ACKNOWLEDGEMENTS

Charcoal drawings by Seán O'Sullivan © National Museum of Ireland.

p. 4. Éamonn Ceannt, HE:EW.2012.1

p. 18. Thomas Clarke, HE:EW.2012.15

p. 30. James Connolly, HE:EW.2012.6

p. 42. Seán Mac Diarmada, HE:EW.2012.7

p. 56. Thomas MacDonagh, HE:EW.2012.13

p. 70. Patrick Pearse, HE:EW.2012.14

p. 90. Joseph Plunkett, HE:EW.2012.18

ACKNOWLEDGEMENTS

The editors would like to thank all of the people involved in this project. Without their support, this book would not have become a reality. The board of the Irish Family History Foundation agreed to commemorate the 1916 Rising by funding and supporting the research into the family histories of the seven signatories of the Proclamation of the Irish Republic. The research of Paul Gorry in compiling this valuable contribution to the 1916/2016 programme of commemorations has been outstanding. Seán O'Sullivan's portraits of the seven signatories are reproduced courtesy of the National Museum of Ireland. All other images are courtesy of Kildare Library Services.

The County Kildare Decade of Commemorations Committee has enabled us to bring this publication to the widest possible audience. We want to acknowledge the support and assistance of the Kildare County Co-ordinator Marian Higgins, the Chair of the County Kildare Commemorations Committee, Cllr. Pádraig McEvoy, Mario Corrigan, Kildare Local Studies Librarian and James Durney, County Kildare Historian in Residence 2016.

Thanks are also due to Conor, Fiona and the staff at Merrion Press for the design of the book.

Karel Kiely and Aisling Dermody, editors

FOREWORD

In the centenary year of the 1916 Rising it is fitting that we examine the origins and backgrounds of the seven men that signed their names to the Proclamation of the Irish Republic.

On Easter Monday, 24 April 1916 at the General Post Office (GPO) in Dublin, the leaders of the Rising proclaimed a free Irish Republic in which the egalitarian idea was centrally enshrined. The Proclamation was read out by Patrick Pearse on the steps of the GPO just after noon; it declared the rights of the people of Ireland to be sovereign and looked forward to the establishment of a native Government elected on the democratic principles of self-determination and government by consent.

The 1916 Rising began the process that led to the separation of Ireland from Great Britain. The people involved in the 1916 Rising envisaged a country that 'guarantees religious and civil liberty, equal rights and equal opportunities to all its citizens, and [which] declares its resolve to pursue the happiness and prosperity of the whole nation and all of its parts, cherishing all of the children of the nation equally.' They believed that this could be achieved only through complete independence.

The Irish Family History Foundation is a network of thirty-four county genealogy centres on the island of Ireland that have been providing a local research service to people at home and abroad for over thirty years. The Foundation engaged genealogist Paul Gorry to research the seven signatories to the Proclamation and their families as part of its contribution to the commemoration of the events of 100 years ago. Kildare County Council and the Kildare Decade of Commemorations are delighted to assist in supporting this publication which is a unique souvenir of the 1916/2016 commemorations that have been so extraordinary in Co. Kildare and Ireland.

Peter Carey
Chief Executive
Kildare County Council

COUNTY KILDARE DECADE OF
COMMEMORATIONS

The centennial year 2016 offered a unique opportunity for exploring and learning the history of our country. The Ireland 2016 programme included a particular focus on the involvement of children and schools, including inviting schools to engage in a project to trace a family tree back to 1916. This was intended to give students a real experience researching archival material and to afford them the opportunity to find out more about the conditions in which people lived in 1916. Completed projects were uploaded to Scoilnet and publicly available for people to browse.

In Co. Kildare we have delivered hundreds of talks to school children at primary and secondary level, taking artefacts and uniforms into the classroom in order to bring the events of 1916 to life. Our county programme for young people has included essay and poetry competitions, Proclamation Day ceremonies, plays, and music.

The family histories of the seven signatories to the Proclamation of the Irish Republic in this book show the diverse backgrounds of the men and their families; this publication is useful both as a piece of genealogical research and as a study of how to carry out research using the sources available.

Cllr. Pádraig McEvoy, Chairperson
Kildare Decade of Commemorations Committee

Introduction

This book explores the family histories of the seven signatories of the Proclamation of the Republic. These seven men came from different backgrounds. Their stories touch on twenty counties and reveal the diverse strands of what may be thought of now as a fairly monochrome nineteenth-century Irish society.

The various county databases on Rootsireland.ie played a central role in tracing these seven families, but the research involved other online sources as well as original records and printed material. The records used are indicated throughout the seven family histories and hopefully these examples will illustrate to readers the range of sources available for Irish genealogical research, and in which cases they may be relevant.

The proclamation was a printed document addressed to the people of Ireland by 'The Provisional Government of the Irish Republic'. The seven men whose names were appended to it represented the organisers of the rebellion. The document was read aloud by Patrick Pearse in front of the General Post Office in Dublin on Easter Monday, 24 April 1916. After the week-long insurrection the leaders were tried and fifteen were executed between 3 May and 12 May. These included the seven signatories. From the extreme poverty of James Connolly's childhood to the privileged upbringing of Joseph Plunkett, a strong nationalist passion was the common bond that united these seven very different individuals. For some of them the surviving records do not allow for tracing beyond the immediate generations; for others there is scope for more research.

The seven families were by no means uniformly republican. Some of the signatories had close relatives in the Royal Irish Constabulary and the British Army. Connolly himself had served in the army in Ireland. The Gaelic Revival, beginning two decades before 1916, sparked an interest in the Irish language and introduced some of the signatories to the language as well as beginning their journey towards militant republicanism. But some of them came from families for whom the language was a living thing just a generation before. Emigration had been a theme of the story of Ireland for centuries, but particularly since The Famine in the 1840s. Two of the signatories, Clarke and Connolly, were born overseas and both spent some years living in the USA. On the other hand, MacDonagh and Pearse each had a parent whose immediate roots were in England.

Many people think of nineteenth-century Ireland as being segregated between Catholic and Protestant, with mixed-religion marriages almost unheard of. Clarke and MacDonagh were products of mixed marriages, Connolly, MacDonagh and Plunkett's wives were born into Church of Ireland families, while Pearse's father was a convert to Catholicism.

The family histories of the seven signatories reveal the diversity of Irish society in the nineteenth century and illustrate its opportunities as well as its limitations. The online sources quoted in the family histories are correct as of 8 February 2016.

Paul Gorry
Member of Accredited Genealogists Ireland

Éamonn Ceannt

Éamonn Ceannt was the commander of the battalion that held the South Dublin Union Workhouse (now St James's Hospital) during the Easter Rising. He was thirty-four years old when he was executed in Kilmainham Gaol on 8 May 1916.

Ceannt was born Edward Thomas Kent in Ballymoe in north-east Co. Galway on 21 September 1881. He spent most of his youth in Co. Louth and the remainder of his life in Dublin. His parents were from Tipperary and Cork. His working career was as a clerk in Dublin Corporation, but his interests drew him increasingly to Irish culture and ultimately to militant republicanism.

According to the *Dictionary of Irish Biography* it was the centenary of the 1798 Rebellion that ignited his interest in cultural nationalism and led him to learn Irish, initially being taught by his father who was a native speaker. Edward Kent adopted the Irish form of his name, Éamonn Ceannt, about this time. Through his involvement with the Gaelic League he met Áine Ní Bhraonáin (born Frances Mary Brennan) and they married on 7 June 1905. They have no living descendants. Their only son Ronan died in 1974.

Éamonn Ceannt did not come from a republican background. His father, James, was a policeman who retired as a Head Constable in 1892. His older brother John also joined the Royal Irish Constabulary in 1889 and served until 1914. His eldest brother William served in the British Army in the Boer War and served as Company Sergeant Major in the Royal Dublin Fusiliers during the Great War, dying in April 1917.

Ceannt's Father's Background

Éamonn Ceannt's father James Kent was born in July 1839, in an area of southern Co. Tipperary bounded on the north by the Galty Mountains and on the south by the Knockmealdowns. James was the third of six identified children of William Kent and Ellen Cleary. He was baptised on 15 July 1839 in Clogheen Roman Catholic parish.

A record of his eldest brother's baptism has not been found. His older sister Mary (12 July 1836) was baptised in Clogheen too, as were his brothers Philip (13 April 1842) and Michael (29 September 1845). His youngest identified sibling, Margaret, was baptised in the adjoining RC parish of Ballyporeen on 11 August 1854. This suggests that the family moved from Clogheen to Ballyporeen between 1845 and 1854.

Unfortunately none of the baptismal entries gives an address. According to James's marriage record his father William was a farmer, but he cannot be found in Griffith's *Primary Valuation* in this district. Clogheen RC parish covers the area of Shanrahan civil parish, while Ballyporeen RC parish covers that of Templetenny. No William Kent appears in either civil parish in Griffith's *Valuation*, which was published for this area in 1852. There were several Kent families there at the time. In Shanrahan civil parish there were six Kent households, in Ballynatona, Curraghslagh, Flemingstown and Shanrahan townlands. In Templetenny civil parish there were three, in Ballywilliam and Skeheenaranky townlands.

As identified by the O'Brien Press *16 Lives* series biography, *Éamonn Ceannt*, written by his grandniece Mary Gallagher, among the Ceannt Papers at the National Library is a transcript of shorthand notes taken down by Éamonn's brother Michael from information spoken to him by his father James.[1] The notes were taken a few months before James's death. James stated that he was born on 14 July 1839 in 'Rehill, near Mitchelstown, County Cork, and four or five miles fro[m] Clogheen, which is the Parish'. He stated that both his parents were born in Rehill, that his father died about 1895 aged ninety-three and his mother died about six years before, aged seventy-six. His father was buried in a graveyard near Shanrahan in which there was an old headstone, inscribed with the name of another William Kent, which was mostly illegible in the 1890s. He referred to his siblings Bill ('four years older than me'), Mary ('two years later'), Philip, Michael ('considered the finest man of the Kents') and Margaret ('now 55 years of age'). Michael emigrated to America but returned on a visit 'about fifteen years ago.'

Rehill is a townland mainly in the civil parish of Shanrahan (Clogheen Roman Catholic) and partly in that of Tubbrid (Ballylooby Roman Catholic), Co. Tipperary, and not exactly close to Mitchelstown. There is no reference to either Kent or Cleary in Rehill in the Tithe Applotment or Griffith's *Valuation*.

According to an endnote in Mary Gallagher's book,[2] a newspaper cutting of a letter by James G. Skinner in the *Irish Press* in 1932, also in the Ceannt Papers, indicates that the family farmed in 'Lyrefune, a townland of Ballyporeen, Co. Tipperary.' This information about Lyrefune is interesting. This townland is in Templetenny civil and Ballyporeen Roman Catholic parish, so presumably they moved there before the birth of Margaret in 1854. Again, no Kent appears in Lyrefune in Griffith's *Valuation*. However, in later years Philip Kent and his sister Margaret lived in Lyrefune. On 5 March 1878 Philip Kent of Lyrefune married Catherine Condon of Glenacunna and his father was stated as William Kent. There is, perhaps, scope for further research on this family.

As already mentioned, Éamonn Ceannt's father James was a native Irish speaker. It is interesting to note that according to the 1911 Census many of the older people in the Ballyporeen area spoke Irish and English.

Ceannt's Mother's Background

Éamonn Ceannt's mother, Johanna Galway, was born about 1840, in northern Co. Cork. Her father was John Galway, described as a steward on the civil record of Johanna's marriage. At the time of her marriage she was described as a seamstress and her address was given as Buttevant. After that there is some uncertainty about Johanna Galway's background.

Firstly, there is the discrepancy about the records of her marriage to James Kent in 1870. There are three separate records of this marriage. The civil record shows that James Kent married 'Johanna Gallway' on 5 July 1870 in Ballyhea Roman Catholic chapel.[3] Both were of full age, previously unmarried and resident in Buttevant. His occupation was stated as 'Police': hers as 'Samestress'. His father was stated as William Kent, a farmer: hers as John Gallway, a steward. The witnesses were Edmond Galway and Kate Galway, and apparently the bride signed her name as 'Johanna Galway'. Lastly, Jeremiah D. Russell, C.C., was the celebrant.

The Rootsireland.ie database pointed to two church records of this marriage, both verified by reference to the microfilmed Roman Catholic parish registers now online. One is in the Ballyhea parish register and the other in that of the adjoining Buttevant parish. Both are dated 8 January 1870. The record in Ballyhea shows that James Kent married 'Joan Galway', with the witnesses stated as Redmond Galway and David Lynch. The entry is initialled 'JR', corresponding to Jeremiah Russell. Above it is written 'from Buttevant' and 'De Buttevant' followed by what appears to be 'cum lecenca Paraoti'. This is most likely a misspelling of 'cum licentia parochi' which roughly translates as 'with the permission of the Parish Priest.'

The entry in the Buttevant parish register shows that James Kent married 'Johanna Gallway', with the witnesses stated as

Edmund Gallway and Mary Gallway. It would appear that the marriage took place on 8 January 1870 in Ballyhea, with Rev. Jeremiah Russell performing the ceremony. Possibly it was recorded also in Buttevant parish because the Parish Priest had given permission for two residents of his parish to marry elsewhere. Presumably when the civil record was returned months later an error was made with the date. In the three records of this marriage a different second witness was given in each case, while the first witness was Edmond/ Edmund or Redmond Galway. In what appears to be the original record he is entered as Redmond.

Searching the Mallow Heritage Centre's database (covering Co. Cork, North & East) on Rootsireland.ie, only one John Galway was found as having a daughter named Johanna in the 1830s/1840s. It would be tempting to accept this Johanna, daughter of John Galway and Mary Barry, baptised in Shandrum parish on 23 May 1841, as Éamonn Ceannt's mother, but the name Redmond Galway presents a doubt.

Shandrum parish does not adjoin Buttevant. It is north of it, straddling the border with Co. Limerick. Of the 1830s/1840s baptisms of children with a father named John Galway, none was in Buttevant parish. The marriage of John Galway to Mary Barry took place in Buttevant parish on 17 February 1835. He was described as 'of Ballyhea'. However, all the identified children of John Galway and Mary Barry were baptised in Shandrum. They were Catherine (1837), Patrick (1839), Johanna (1841), Ellen (1844) and Mary (1846). The address 'Curragh' on some of these baptisms would seem to correspond to Curraghcloonabro East in

Shandrum civil parish, where a John Galway was recorded in Griffith's *Valuation*. He had a house only, valued at 12 shillings.

The only other John Galway in Griffith's *Valuation* in the general area of Buttevant was in Castleharrison in Ballyhay civil parish (covered by Ballyhea RC parish). He was renting buildings valued at £2-15-0 and 3½ acres of land from S. H. Harrison, Esquire. Going back to the 1830s/1840s baptisms of children with a father named John Galway, there are entries in Ballyhea Roman Catholic parish. John Galway and Catherine Carroll had three children baptised there – John (1834), Redmond (1837) and Michael (1841). This baptism in 1837 is the only one in the database about that time for a Redmond Galway. In 1901 and 1911 Redmond Galway was living in Castleharrison. In 1901 his brother Richard was there. As the baptisms of the three identified children of John Galway and Catherine Carroll are separated by a few years, it is possible that the Ballyhea register has omissions. Certainly there is no entry for Richard so it is possible that there was another child named Johanna. More in-depth research would be needed to confirm Éamonn Ceannt's mother's parentage.

Ceannt's Immediate Family

On 15 January 1862, at the stated age of twenty-one, Éamonn Ceannt's father James Kent joined the Irish Constabulary (it gained its Royal designation in 1867).[4] He was recommended by Rev. P. De Burke, then Parish Priest of

Ballyporeen. James's first posting was to East Cork on 13 May 1862. It was while there, apparently stationed at Buttevant, that James Kent married Johanna Galway in 1870. James was promoted in 1871 to Assistant Constable. The first few years of their married life were spent in Buttevant, but their third child was baptised in the adjoining Roman Catholic parish of Ballyclough. It was possibly just before his transfer out of Cork that James Kent was promoted to Constable (or sergeant). In October 1873 he was transferred to Galway. For the next decade the family lived in Ballymoe in the north-east of Co. Galway, near its border with Roscommon. It was here that Johanna Kent gave birth to her five youngest children, including Éamonn. In October 1883 James Kent was promoted to Head Constable and two months later he was transferred to Co. Louth. Apparently he was stationed in Ardee and later Drogheda. James retired on pension in April 1892.

About that time the family moved to Dublin, where they lived at a number of addresses in the North Strand/Fairview/ Drumcondra area of the city. When Johanna Kent, Éamonn's mother, died on 16 February 1895 they were living at 26 Bayview Avenue. She was buried in Glasnevin Cemetery.[5] By 1901 the family home was 23 Fairview Avenue.[6] At the time of the 1911 Census James Kent, described as a house agent, was living with his daughter and her husband at 13 St Alphonsus Road.[7] That was still his address when he died the following year, on St Patrick's Day. He was buried with his wife in Glasnevin. Probate of his will was granted on 31 August 1912 to his sons Michael J., Edward T. (Éamonn) and Richard Kent. His effects were valued at £455-2-2.[8]

James Kent and Johanna Galway had eight children:

1. William Kent; born in Buttevant, 20 December 1870; baptised in Buttevant Roman Catholic parish, 26 December. He has been identified with the William Leeman Kent who had a career in the Royal Dublin Fusiliers. This man was a sergeant in the regiment in 1911, when he was stationed at Naas, Co. Kildare. The 1911 Census shows him as born in Co. Cork, aged thirty-five and unmarried. Company Sergeant Major William Leeman Kent died on the Western Front on 24 April 1917 and was commemorated on the Arras Memorial.[9] This William Leeman Kent's birthplace is said to be Buttevant. This search has not established for certain that this man was indeed Éamonn Ceannt's brother.

2. John Patrick Kent; born in Buttevant, 16 December 1871; baptised in Buttevant Roman Catholic parish, 20 December. He joined the RIC on 25 October 1889, recommended by District Inspector Sharpe.[10] He was posted to Co. Wicklow in 1890 and was stationed in Rathdrum in 1901. He spent a few months in 1901–2 in the reserve on Co. Roscommon before returning to Wicklow, presumably the Stratford area. On 8 October 1907 in Dublin he married Elizabeth Cummins from Stratford. Two months later he was transferred to Co. Kildare. He was stationed at Robertstown in 1911. He remained in Kildare until he was pensioned in November 1914,

when he appears to have returned to live in Stratford. After eight years of marriage Elizabeth gave birth in April 1916 to their only child, a daughter named Johanna Mary (Joan). A few days later Elizabeth became seriously ill and died on Easter Sunday as the rebellion was about to begin.[11] Later John was a civil servant. At the time of his death his address was 24 Belvedere Road, Dublin. He died on 13 April 1949 and was buried in the family plot in Glasnevin.

3. Ellen Kent; born 20 May 1873; baptised in Ballyclough Roman Catholic parish, 23 May. Apparently after her mother's death she kept house for her father. On 27 April 1908 at St Agatha's Roman Catholic church, North William Street, Dublin, she married John Joseph Casey, a law clerk. They were living with her father in 1911 at 13 St Alphonsus Road and they remained there after his death. It would appear that they had no children. She died as a widow on 2 June 1939 and was buried in the Kent family plot in Glasnevin.

4. James Charles Kent; born in Ballymoe, 29 October 1875. He was living in the family home, 23 Fairview Avenue, in 1901, described as an assistant house agent. He died unmarried on 13 April 1905. His address at that time was 232 Clonliffe Road and he was a mercantile clerk. He was buried in the family plot in Glasnevin.

5. Michael Kent; born in Ballymoe, 26 November 1877; died as an infant in 1878. It was a common practice

when a child died young to give the same name to the next child of the same sex, born relatively soon afterwards. The Kents gave this son's name to their next boy.

6. Michael Kent; born in Ballymoe, 15 April 1879. He was living in the family home in 1901, described as a typist. On 24 August 1910 he married Julia Gibney, who was born in Co. Wicklow. In 1911 they were living at 54 Drumcondra Road Lower, and he was a Dublin Corporation official. They had at least two children, Johanna (Joan, born 1911) and Alice (born 1913). Their granddaughter Mary Gallagher wrote the Éamonn Ceannt volume in the O'Brien Press *16 Lives* biography series.

7. Edward Thomas Kent (Éamonn Ceannt); born in Ballymoe, 21 September 1881.

8. Richard Kent; born in Ballymoe, 22 May 1883. He was living in the family home in 1901, then a seventeen-year-old student. On 17 August 1909 he married Anastatia Dillon in her native Co. Kerry. In 1911 they were living at 69 Richmond Road, Dublin, and he was a second division clerk in the Irish Land Commission. It would appear that they had at least one child, Kathleen (born 1912).

Ceannt's Wife's Background

Ceannt married Áine Ní Bhraonáin at St James's Roman Catholic parish church in Dublin on 7 June 1905.[12] Though they signed the civil record under their adopted Irish names they were also recorded as Edward T. Kent and Frances M. Brennan. At the time of the 1911 Census[13] they were living at 4 Herberton Lane in Kilmainham with their four-year-old son Ronan as well as Áine's sister 'Eilís' (Lily) and her mother Elizabeth. Ceannt completed the census in Irish, with the exception of his mother-in-law's name and her place of birth, England.

At the time of the Easter Rising Ceannt's address was 2 Dolphin Terrace, South Circular Road. Administration of his estate, with the will annexed, was granted to his widow 'Frances Kent' on 18 November 1916, his effects amounting to £290-6-2.[14]

Both Áine and her sister Lily received their own entries in the *Dictionary of Irish Biography*. According to these their father, Francis Brennan, was an auctioneer and allegedly a former Fenian. However, on the civil record of his marriage to Elizabeth Butler in 1874 he was described simply as a shopkeeper. He was a widower living at 11 South Richmond Street, Dublin, when he married Elizabeth and his parents were recorded as Maurice Brennan, a merchant, and Elizabeth Biel of Liverpool. Francis and Elizabeth married at St James's Roman Catholic church on 12 May 1874.[15] She was staying at 170 James Street and her parents were recorded as John Butler, a shopkeeper, and Elizabeth Byrne of Tramore. However, according to the 1901 Census Elizabeth herself was born in Manchester about 1850. Her mother was living with her in 1901 and her county of birth was stated as Waterford.

The family lived in South Richmond Street up to at least 1876, in North Summer Street in 1878, and in Upper Camden Street in 1880. Francis Brennan died before the 1901 Census, at which time his widow Elizabeth was a ward mistress in the South Dublin Union (the institution her future son-in-law later occupied during the Easter Rising). She had accommodation in the workhouse complex, where she lived with her mother and her daughters 'Elizabeth' (Lily) and 'Frances' (Áine).[16]

Francis Brennan and Elizabeth Butler had four children:

1. Mary J. Brennan; baptised in Rathmines Roman Catholic parish, 20 June 1875; apparently died young.

2. Catherine M. Brennan (Kathleen O'Brennan); baptised in Rathmines, 26 November 1876; playwright; died in 1948.

3. Elizabeth Mary Brennan (Lily O'Brennan); baptised in St Mary's Pro Cathedral Roman Catholic parish, 4 September 1878; writer and political activist; died in 1948.

4. Frances Mary Brennan (Áine Ní Bhraonáin); baptised apparently in St Kevin's Roman Catholic church, Harrington Street, 24 September 1880; political activist and executive of the Irish Red Cross; wife of Éamonn Ceannt; died in 1954. Her only child Ronan died in 1974.

Éamonn Ceannt's widow, Áine, his sister Ellen Casey and his son Ronan successfully claimed Military Service pensions in respect of his activities.[17]

Thomas Clarke

Thomas Clarke was the oldest of the seven signatories. He had joined the IRB as a young man, before going to work in New York. In 1883 he went on a bombing mission to England, where he was arrested. After his release in 1898 he moved to Dublin for a while before returning to the USA. In 1907 he again moved to Dublin, where he was co-opted on to the IRB supreme council. He was fifty-eight years old when he was executed in Kilmainham Gaol on 3 May 1916.

Clarke was born on 11 March 1858 at Hurst Castle in Hampshire, on the south coast of England. His father, James Clarke, was stationed there at the time as a bombardier in the Royal Artillery Regiment. Louis N. Le Roux's 1936 biography of Clarke states that Thomas's widow had a certificate relating to James Clarke indicating that he was born in 1830 in the parish of Carrigallen, Co. Leitrim, and that he was a member of the Church of Ireland. The reference is vague but it appears to refer to a baptismal certificate.[18] According to Helen Litton's biography *Thomas Clarke*, in the O'Brien Press *16 Lives* series, James Clarke was from Errew townland, Carrigallen, Co. Leitrim, and was born in 1830, son of James Clarke or Clerkin, who shared a small farm with his brother

Owen, and the family was Protestant. No source is quoted for this information.

Thomas Clarke's mother was Mary Palmer, who married James Clarke in 1857 in Shanrahan, Co. Tipperary. Helen Litton cites 'Notes for a Life of Tom Clarke' in the Clarke Papers at the National Library[19] as stating that Mary Palmer's mother's maiden surname was Kew and that her funeral in the 1880s was a big public occasion.

Le Roux and Litton give accounts of James Clarke's military career and of the family's travels. Before his marriage James fought in the Crimean War, serving at the battles of Alma, Balaklava and Ickerman and the siege of Sebastopol. When Thomas, the eldest child, was a year old the family went to the Cape of Good Hope (now South Africa), where they spent almost six years. Returning to Ireland, James was appointed to the Tyrone Artillery Militia and the family settled in Dungannon, Co. Tyrone. It was here that Thomas Clarke grew to maturity.

Clarke's Father's Background

James Clarke's marriage record and the records of his career in the British Army appear to be the only documentary sources for his origin. His marriage to Mary Palmer was in Shanrahan Church of Ireland parish church on 21 May 1857, when he was stationed in Clonmel. The marriage record states that his father was James Clarke, a labourer.[20] His army record shows that he joined the Royal Artillery Regiment at Ballyshannon, Co. Donegal, on 4 December 1847 at the stated age of seventeen years and eleven months. It states that he was born in Carrigallen parish, near Carrigallen, Co. Leitrim, and at the time he was a groom by trade.[21]

It is worth noting that young men often enlisted in the army at a location some distance from home. However, Ballyshannon was a considerable distance from Carrigallen by road, particularly in the 1840s. Other garrison towns would have been more accessible from Carrigallen. This suggests the possibility that, before enlisting, James had found work as a groom closer to Ballyshannon, or indeed that his family had moved in that direction.

Errew is a townland in Carrigallen civil parish, south of Carrigallen town and on the shore of Gulladoo Lough. This is in the most easterly part of the province of Connacht. Errew is about two miles from where Connacht, Leinster and Ulster meet. In the Tithe Applotment Book for Carrigallen parish (1830s) there is, indeed, an entry under 'Erew' for 'James Clerkin & Owen Clerkin', together holding six Irish acres. This would appear to be Helen Litton's source for the Errew connection. By the time of Griffith's *Primary Valuation* (1857) the only Clerkin/Clarke in Errew was Owen Clarke, who held just over eleven statute acres. Owen Clarke was succeeded in his property by his son William. Owen was deceased by 1880, when William married Rose Connolly in Carrigallen Roman Catholic church.[22] The family was Roman Catholic from at least that point forward.

Clerkin and Clarke could have been used interchangeably in this area in the nineteenth century. However, if Errew has been identified as James Clarke's birthplace based merely

on the assumption that his father would have appeared in
the Tithe Applotment, there is nothing to support Errew
as the correct location. James's father James was stated as
a labourer on the 1857 marriage record. Only landholders
can be expected to appear in the Tithes. A labourer with a
small holding would very likely be omitted. Indeed, there
is no certainty about finding landless labourers in the later
Griffith's *Valuation*.

If Le Roux was quoting from James Clarke's baptismal
certificate it would have been helpful if he had given the
full details. The registers of Carrigallen Church of Ireland
parish, dating from 1804, perished in 1922 when the Public
Record Office was destroyed during the Civil War. Nothing
survives before the 1880s. Incidentally, the earliest surviving
Carrigallen Roman Catholic baptismal records cover
November 1829 to February 1830, after which there is a gap
to 1838.

Luckily, in the absence of church records, a copy of the
1821 Census for Carrigallen parish survives. It was
microfilmed by the National Library in the mid-twentieth
century from the copy then in the possession of Mr George
Rosemond, Senior. The microfilm is labelled 'Census of the
parish of Carrigallen, co. Leitrim, *c.*1833 (probably the 1831
Census).'[23] Certainly it is not copied from the 1831 Census,
as that census did not include the names of all household
members. It has been asserted that it was from the 1821
Census. Its pages resemble those of the surviving 1821 returns,
but some of the details are omitted. The copy is annotated
with the letters 'R' or 'P' beside each household, evidently

indicating religious denomination as 'Roman' or 'Protestant'. These details did not appear in the original census.

The only Clarke (or Clerkin) households in this 1821 Census for Carrigallen parish were in Drumbrecanlis ('Drumbrinless'), Errew and Kivvy ('Kivey'), while an Owen Clerke was a lodger in Drumleevan ('Drumlevan'). In each case the denomination was indicated as 'R'. However, the only place the name James Clarke/Clerkin appeared was Errew. There, James Clerke (aged sixty-three) lived with his wife Mary (fifty) and his children Eugane (twenty-six), Peter (twenty-two), James (eighteen), William (sixteen), Edward (twelve), Thomas (twelve) and Judith (nine). Incidentally, the names Owen and Eugene were often used interchangeably. It is possible that the son James (born about 1803) was the grandfather of Thomas Clarke. Unfortunately, the available information on the family is patchy and, concerning religious denomination, contradictory. Further evidence would be needed to draw any definite conclusions.

Clarke's Mother's Background

Thomas Clarke's mother was Mary Palmer, who married James Clarke in the Shanrahan Church of Ireland parish church, Co. Tipperary, on 21 May 1857. Though she married in the Anglican parish church, it was said that she was Roman Catholic. The Roman Catholic parish corresponding to Shanrahan is called Clogheen. The marriage record states that her father was Michael Palmer, a labourer, that she herself was a servant and that she was resident in (the

town of) Clogheen. As related by Helen Litton, when the
Clarkes returned from South Africa Mary had a child born
in Clogheen in 1865, and the informant on his birth record
was Bridget Palmer.

Palmer was not a common surname in Co. Tipperary.
In the extreme south of the county it was quite rare. Within
Clogheen Superintendent Registrar's District (covering the
area from Cahir to the Cork border) from the commencement
of civil registration to the end of the nineteenth century there
were ten Palmer deaths registered, four marriages and no
births.

Michael Palmer did not appear in Griffith's *Valuation*,
but as a labourer he would not necessarily be expected to.
However, it can be stated that he lived within Ballylooby
Roman Catholic parish (covering Tubbrid, Tullaghorton and
Whitechurch civil parishes) in the 1830s and 1840s. He
may have moved into the town of Clogheen later, as he died
there in 1883. However, Clogheen is right at the boundary
between Shanrahan and Tullaghorton civil parishes, so
perhaps he always lived on the outskirts of the town, while
within Ballylooby Roman Catholic parish. Michael Palmer
was probably born in the early 1810s. As he married in
1832 he could not have been as young as sixty-three (his
stated age) when he died in 1883. He died of bronchitis
on 22 May 1883 in Clogheen. His death record described
him as a labourer and his wife Bridget was the informant.[24]
Bridget died in Clogheen three months later, on 31 August
1883.[25] Her stated age of sixty-five was also inaccurate, but
presumably she was born in the 1810s. As she married in

Ballylooby Roman Catholic parish presumably that was also her native place. Bridget's maiden surname was not Kew, as related in the 'Notes for a Life of Tom Clarke'. Interestingly, it was Kent. Éamonn Ceannt's father James Kent was born in 1839 in Clogheen Roman Catholic parish. There were several Kent families in the area and there is no possibility of tracing a relationship, but it can be said that Thomas Clarke and Éamonn Ceannt had a common ancestry.

Michael Palmer married Bridget Kent in Ballylooby Roman Catholic parish on 26 January 1832. They had five known children, all baptised in Ballylooby Roman Catholic parish:

1. James Palmer; baptised 23 November 1832.
2. Mary Palmer; baptised 16 October 1834; married James Clarke and was the mother of Thomas Clarke (see below).
3. Thomas Palmer; baptised 11 December 1837.
4. Johanna or Jane Palmer; baptised 31 October 1841.
5. Alice Palmer; baptised 12 October 1845.

Clarke's Immediate Family

Thomas Clarke's father James Clarke was born about 1830. He joined the British Army in 1847 and served in the Royal Artillery in the Crimean War. Later he was stationed at Clonmel and met his future wife Mary Palmer. After their marriage in 1857 he was transferred to Hampshire, where Thomas was born. A year later he was sent to the Cape of Good Hope, where he re-enlisted for nine years in 1860. After his return to the United Kingdom he was appointed to the Tyrone Artillery Militia in 1865. He claimed his discharge from the army in 1869 and continued in the militia until 1886.

By 1901 Mary Clarke was a widow living at 5 Blessington Place (off Blessington Street), Dublin, where she kept a lodging house. At the time of the 1911 Census she was living with her daughter Hannah in Great Britain Street and she was stated as having had eight children, of whom four were still living. She died on 16 July 1922 in Station Road, Baldoyle, Co. Dublin.

James Clarke and Mary Palmer had eight children:

1. Thomas Clarke; born at Hurst Castle, Hampshire, England, 11 March 1858.

2. Maria Jane Clarke; born in Natal, Cape of Good Hope, 23 December 1859;[26] according to Helen Litton she married Teddy Fleming in 1901 and died in the 1920s, having had a son Edward J. Fleming who corresponded with President de Valera in 1966. It has not been possible to find any record of the Flemings, except to confirm that in 1905 Maria and her husband Ed Fleming were living in the USA in the New York area.[27]

3. unknown name; as the 1911 Census indicated that Mary Clarke had eight children, it is likely that two were born and died between 1860 and 1864, while the family was in the Cape Colony.

4. unknown name.

5. Michael Clarke; born in Clogheen, Co. Tipperary, 9 May 1865; possibly died in infancy, but certainly dead by 1911.

6. Hannah Clarke; born in Dungannon, Co. Tyrone, 24 August 1868; was living with her mother in Blessington Place, Dublin, in 1901; was a tobacconist in Great Britain Street, Dublin, in 1911; died unmarried in the Hospice, Harold's Cross, Dublin, 11 October 1950.[28]

7. Alfred Edward Clarke; born in Dungannon, 24 May 1870; was living with his mother in Blessington Place, Dublin, in 1901, when his occupation was time-keeper; married about 1902–3 Emily (born in Limerick about 1880–1); lived in London for some years but returned to Dublin and apparently resumed his job as a time-keeper for Dublin Corporation. By 1911 his wife had four children but three were still alive. Alfred was living at 18 Michael's Hill, Dublin, in 1911, with his wife and three children. Helen Litton stated that Alfred went missing in November 1917 and his body was found in the Grand Canal. He was survived by his wife and five children. Alfred and Emily had at least six children,[29] James (b. London about 1903–4), John (b. London about 1905–6), Nora (b. London about 1907–8), a child who died by 1911, Emily and Thomas.

8. Joseph George Clarke; born in Northland Row, Dungannon, 16 November 1874; died six days later on 22 November.[30]

Clarke's Wife's Background

Clarke's wife, Kathleen Daly, came from a prominent republican family from Limerick. Her uncle, John Daly, visited Dungannon in 1878 as an organiser for the IRB and he had a big influence on the young Clarke. After Clarke was released from prison in 1898 he was given the freedom of the city of Limerick in 1899, where Daly was Mayor at the time. On this occasion he met his future wife, who was twenty years younger than him. They married in New York on 16 July 1901.

Kathleen Daly was born on 12 April 1878 in Henry Street, Limerick, to Edward Daly and Catherine/Kathleen O'Mara. Edward Daly was a timber measurer at the time, and when he died he was the harbour weigh master. He died on 9 September 1890 in Frederick Street (now O'Curry Street), Limerick, at the stated aged of forty-one.[31] His parents, John Daly and Margaret Hayes, married in St Michael's Roman Catholic parish in February 1833. They had six children, including John (baptised in St Munchin's Roman Catholic parish in October 1845) and Edward (baptised in St Munchin's in May 1848).[32]

Edward Daly had married Catherine O'Mara in St Michael's Roman Catholic church, Limerick, on 18 January 1873. Her father was Daniel O'Mara, a coachman. Edward and Catherine had nine daughters born before Edward's premature death. Catherine gave birth to their tenth child and first son six months after Edward died. He was named John Edward or 'Ned'. He was destined to play his part in

O'Connell (Sackville) Street, Dublin, before the insurrection. All images courtesy of Kildare Library Services.

O'Connell (Sackville) Street, Dublin, from O'Connell Bridge, after the bombardment.

General view of ruins from O'Connell Bridge, Dublin, after the bombardment.

[1917 ISSUE]

Compiled by the "*WEEKLY IRISH TIMES*," Dublin.

SINN FEIN REBELLION HANDBOOK.

Easter, 1916.

A Complete and Connected Narrative of the Rising, with Detailed Accounts of the Fighting at All Points.

Story of the Great Fires, with List of Premises Involved.

Military and Rebel Proclamations and Despatches.

Punishment of Rebels—Full Record of Sentences.

Casualties—Official Lists of Military, Royal Irish Constabulary, Dublin Metropolitan Police, Volunteer Training Corps, and Rebels.

Names of Persons Interred in Cemeteries.

Official Lists of Prisoners Deported and Released.

SPECIAL MAP PRINTED IN COLOURS
(*Illustrating the Area of Fighting*).

Despatches of Sir John Maxwell and Viscount French.

Honours, Promotions and Awards to Military, Police, and Civilians.

Courts-martial at Richmond Barracks—Reports of Public Trials.

Sir Roger Casement's Landing, Capture, Trial and Execution.

Hardinge Commission of Inquiry—Evidence and Report.

Simon Commission of Inquiry—Evidence and Report.

Work of the Hospitals—St. John Ambulance—City and County of Dublin Red Cross Societies—Lists of Names.

Facsimile Reproductions of Rebel Proclamations, &c.

Names of Prisoners Released under General Amnesty.

Photographs, Personal Notes, and Index.

PRICE 1/6 NET.

POSTAGE FOURPENCE.

Sinn Fein Rebellion Handbook title page.

Henry Street, Dublin, showing the side of the GPO, Coliseum and Arnott's.

Henry Street, Dublin, after the shelling of the rebels, May 1916.

Royal Hibernian Academy & Wynn's Hotel, Abbey Street, Dublin.

Corner of Abbey Street, Dublin.

Irish War News, April 1916 (from souvenir booklet *Dublin After the Six Days' Insurrection*).

Inside the General Post Office, Dublin.

O'Connell (Sackville) Street, Dublin, showing the ruins of Hotel Metropole & the GPO.

Irish Rebellion_ May 1916
Sackville Street in flames_ A Photograph taken by a
"Daily Sketch" Photographer under fire

O'Connell (Sackville) Street, Dublin, in flames.

Corner of O'Connell (Sackville) Street, and Eden Quay (from souvenir booklet *The Rebellion in Dublin*).

After the insurrection: the west side of Lower O'Connell (Sackville) Street, Dublin, showing the ruins of Hotel Metropole.

the 1916 Rising, and to die by execution, aged twenty-five, the day after Clarke. Ned is the subject of the *Edward Daly* biography in the O'Brien Press *16 Lives* series, also written by Helen Litton, who is his and Kathleen's grandniece.

After Thomas Clarke's execution Kathleen played a prominent political role, serving as a TD, a senator and the first female Lord Mayor of Dublin. She died in England in September 1972.

Clarke's Children

Thomas Clarke and Kathleen Daly had three children:

1. John Daly ('Daly') Clarke; born in New York, 13 June 1902; married in Dublin, 1952, Mary Byrne. According to Helen Litton, he had no children and died in 1971.
2. Thomas James ('Tom') Clarke; born in William Street, Limerick, 3 March 1908; married in Dublin, 1939, Maureen Kennedy. According to Helen Litton, he had no children and died in 1988.
3. Edward Emmet ('Emmet') Clarke; born in Dublin, 13 August 1909; married in Dublin, 1955, Ellen Mullaney. According to Helen Litton, he moved to Nottingham and later Liverpool. Died in 2004, having had two sons.

James Connolly

James Connolly was the socialist revolutionary among the seven signatories. He had come to Ireland from his native Scotland in 1896 as an organiser for the Dublin Socialist Club. Previously he had served in the British Army and apparently was stationed for a time in Ireland. In Dublin he helped found the Irish Socialist Republican Party. Connolly spent the years 1903 to 1910 in the USA. Returning to Dublin, he became involved in the Irish Transport and General Workers Union. During the 1913 Lockout he was one of the founders of the Irish Citizen Army, one of the groups that participated in the Easter Rising. He was nearly forty-seven years old when he was executed in Kilmainham Gaol on 12 May 1916.

Connolly was born on 5 June 1868 at 107 Cowgate, a long street on the lower level of Edinburgh's Old Town. Cowgate was then a crowded area housing many Irish migrants. Connolly's parents, John Connolly and Mary McGinn, were born in Ireland but they had lived in Edinburgh since at least the mid-1850s. The *Dictionary of Irish Biography* states that they both were born 'in 1833, possibly in Co. Monaghan' but the year can only be based on their stated ages in later life.

It would appear that Connolly knew little of his family history as he was the informant on the death records of both his parents and gave what appears to have been inaccurate information on their parentage. It is probable that he believed that his parents were from Monaghan, as he gave that county as his own birthplace in both the 1901 and 1911 Censuses of Ireland, though he clearly knew that he was born in Edinburgh.

Connolly's Parents' Background

The earliest definite record of Connolly's parents that has been found is that of their marriage. They were married, after banns, on 20 October 1856 by Rev. Alexander O'Donnell at 17 Brown Square, Edinburgh. This was Father O'Donnell's residence. He was one of the priests at St Patrick's, Cowgate.[33] A decade later the square was demolished and its site became part of Chambers Street. It was relatively close to Connolly's birthplace in Cowgate. According to the marriage record, John Connolly and Mary McGinn were both aged twenty-three, previously unmarried and living at 6 Kings Stables, Grassmarket. This area was adjacent to Cowgate and below Edinburgh Castle.

The marriage record stated that John Connolly was an agricultural labourer, which suggests that he was not long in the city. His parents were stated as John Connolly, labourer, deceased, and Mary Connolly, maiden name Markie. Mary McGinn was stated as a domestic servant and her parents as James McGinn, labourer and Maria

McGinn, deceased, maiden surname Burns. It would appear that the bride and groom signed their names, while their witnesses, Myles Clark and Mary Carthy, were unable to do so.

It may be assumed that John and Mary gave their parents' names to the priest and indicated that his father and her mother were deceased. People were rarely accurate with their ages in the nineteenth century but, as the bride and groom were recorded as aged twenty-three, it is likely that they were born approximately in 1833. The ages they gave in the 1861, 1871 and 1881 Census returns were relatively consistent. They suggest that John was born about 1832–4 and that Mary was born about 1833–7.

On Rootsireland.ie it is possible to do a search across all databases, which cover most parts of Ireland. Not knowing for sure whether John Connolly and Mary McGinn, or either of them, originated in Co. Monaghan, this was the only real option for trying to identify a baptismal record. The search was not limited to John and Mary. It covered any child of John Connolly and Mary Markie, or James McGinn/Maginn and Maria/Mary Burnes/Byrne. Allowance was made for variant spellings of names (e.g. Maria/Mary; Markie/Markey; McGinn/Maginn; Burns/Byrne). No child of either couple was found. The most likely explanation is that both families were from parishes for which the surviving baptismal registers do not go back far enough. Indeed, it is worth noting that none of the twenty Roman Catholic parishes in Co. Monaghan have surviving baptismal records pre-dating 1835.

Of James Connolly's four grandparents' surnames, the most localised is Markie (more usually spelled Markey). As MacLysaght's *The Surnames of Ireland* indicates, this is a name associated with the area of the ancient territory of Oriel (generally south Ulster and north Leinster). Matheson's 'Special Report on Surnames in Ireland', using the births recorded in 1890 as an indicator, shows that Markey was principally found in Cos. Monaghan and Dublin.[34]

No evidence has been found of Connolly's grandparents living in Edinburgh. James McGinn was not positively identified there in the 1851 or 1861 Census returns. Certainly Connolly's parents were not living with an extended family in 1861, 1871 or 1881. It has been possible to follow the lives of John and Mary Connolly through the latter half of the nineteenth century through census returns and civil records on Scotlandspeople.gov.uk. They remained in 6 Kings Stable until at least January 1862. In 1865 and 1866 they were living in Campbell's Close, Cowgate. James Connolly himself was born in Cowgate in 1868, but by 1871 they were living at 45 Carrubbers Close, one of the narrow 'closes' leading downhill off the Royal Mile. In 1881 they were back to their old neighbourhood, at 2A Kings Stables. Mary died in 1892 at 15 Alison's Close, Cowgate, and when John died in 1900 his address was in Lawnmarket.

John Connolly apparently came to Edinburgh as an agricultural labourer, so the occupations open to him were limited. He had various jobs through the years. He was a railway carter, a manure carter, a lamplighter, a city public lavatory attendant, and at various times, simply described as a carter.

James Connolly's mother Mary died in Alison's Close on 16 May 1892, having suffered from chronic bronchitis for some thirty years and acute bronchitis for two months. She also suffered for an unknown duration from mitral incompetence, meaning that the mitral valve did not close properly when blood was pumped out of the heart. There was no medical attendant, and this information was given by her son James when he registered her death. He stated that her parents were James McGinn, agricultural labourer, and Susan McGinn, maiden name Burns, both deceased. All details except for her mother's first name are consistent with the information on her marriage record. He stated that she was fifty-four (born about 1837–8) but based on her other estimates of birth she was likely a few years older.

Connolly's father John died at the Royal Infirmary on 20 April 1900 from a cerebral haemorrhage. Again, James was the informant on the death record and the stated age was sixty-four (born about 1835–6), another apparent underestimate. John's parents were stated as Owen Connolly, farm labourer, and Catherine Connolly, maiden name McBride, both deceased. These names were entirely at odds with the information given on his marriage record. It is much more likely that the information given on the marriage record was correct. Nevertheless, the alternative parents' names given for Mary and John by their son were also checked on the Rootsireland.ie database, with negative results.

John Connolly married Mary McGinn in Edinburgh on 20 October 1856. They had five known children, all born in Edinburgh:

1. Margaret Connolly; born at 6 Kings Stables, 1 or 2 January 1859; baptised in St Mary's Roman Catholic Cathedral, 2 January 1859; died 1861.
2. John Connolly; born at 6 Kings Stables, 31 January 1862. According to the *16 Lives* biography of James Connolly, John served in the British Army in India and on his return in the late 1880s he became involved in the labour movement in Dundee.[35]
3. Mary Connolly; born 15 July 1864; baptised in St Patrick's Roman Catholic church, 31 July 1864; died in Campbell's Close, Cowgate, 29 May 1865, of rubeola (or measles) and bronchitis.
4. Thomas Connolly; born in Campbell's Close, 27 April 1866; living at home with his parents in 1881 as a fifteen-year-old apprentice compositor.
5. James Connolly; born at 107 Cowgate, 5 June 1868.

Connolly's Wife's Background

It is said that Connolly met Lillie Reynolds in Dublin while he was serving in the British Army in Ireland. After he returned to Scotland, Lillie joined him there and they married on 30 April 1890 in the Roman Catholic church in Perth, though she was from a Church of Ireland family. According to Lorcan Collins in his biography of Connolly, Lillie and her twin sister Margaret were born in Carnew, Co. Wicklow, in 1867 to parents named John and Margaret. John, a farm labourer, is said to have died at a young age and Margaret moved to Dublin with her two daughters and two sons, John and George, settling in the Rathmines area. Lillie's twin, Margaret, was living with her husband Jack in Edinburgh in July 1898, at which time they had no children.[36]

According to the 1901 and 1911 Census returns, Lillie was indeed born in Co. Wicklow about 1867–8. Her marriage record gives the same estimate of birth and gives her parents as John Reynolds, farm labourer, and Margaret Reynolds, maiden name Newman, both deceased. Though Lillie used no other first name during her adult life, Lillie was normally a pet name for Elizabeth and it is likely that this was her full name.

It is possible that Lillie and her family lived in Carnew for a time but it would appear that she was not born there. It is probable, also, that she was about four years older than the census returns stated. It is very unlikely that she was born during the period of civil registration (1864 forward). Whether she and Margaret were twins has not been established, but it is probable that her brothers George and John were twins.

There is scope for research on Lillie Connolly's background. For now a vague outline of the family's possible background can be sketched. In Dunganstown Church of Ireland parish, in south-east Co. Wicklow, a John Reynolds married Mary Magee on 30 January 1840. They would appear to have been the parents of two children baptised in the same parish,

George (b. October 1840; baptised 6 August 1841) and James (b. 22 September 1842; baptised 8 January 1843). In both cases the parents were John and Mary Reynolds of Kilcandra and the father was described as a labourer.

Also in Dunganstown Church of Ireland parish, on 20 October 1857 John Reynolds of 'Coniamstown', labourer, a forty-two-year-old widower, married Margaret Kilby of the same townland, a servant aged thirty-two and single. Cunniamstown Big and Cunniamstown Little are adjoining townlands in Dunganstown civil parish and they are about four miles east of the town of Rathdrum. Kilcandra townland adjoins Cunniamstown Big.

Lillie Connolly's parents were John Reynolds and Margaret Newman. No record of the marriage of a couple of these names has emerged. This raises the possibility that Margaret Newman, for some reason, married under the surname Kilby. Two further potentially relevant baptisms were identified. In Dunganstown Church of Ireland parish, Margaret Maria daughter of John Reynolds, labourer, and his wife Margaret was baptised on 16 June 1861 (born 16 May). In Rathdrum Church of Ireland parish, Eliza Jane daughter of John Reynolds, farmer, and his wife Margaret, of Fairview Ballylough was baptised on 14 February 1864 (born 20 December 1863). Fairview was the name of a house in the small townland of Keeloges in Kilcommon civil parish, east of Rathdrum town. Keeloges also adjoins Cunniamstown Big.

The foregoing is an outline of the family's *possible* background. The following is what is known for certain about Lillie Connolly's family.

John Reynolds married Margaret Newman. John was dead by November 1884, when his son George converted to Catholicism. Margaret was dead by April 1890, when her daughter Lillie married. John and Margaret had four known children:

1. Margaret Reynolds; possibly the Margaret Maria baptised in Dunganstown on 16 June 1861; living with her husband Jack in Edinburgh in July 1898.

2. George Reynolds; born about 1861–3 (in Rathdrum, according to the 1911 Census); converted to Catholicism in St Kevin's Church, Harrington Street, Dublin, 15 November 1884, at which time he gave his date of birth as 29 May 1861; living in Ryan's Buildings, Charlemont Street, in 1885–8; was a clockmaker living in Charlemont Mall, Dublin, in 1901 and 1911. He married firstly at St Kevin's, 26 July 1885, Bridget Wheatley, and had at least two children by her, Mary Jane (1886) and William Joseph (1888). He married secondly at St Kevin's, 16 April 1899, Margaret Nolan, and had at least seven children by her, John (1900), George (1901), Eveline (1903), Kathleen (1905), Ernest (1907), Charles (1909) and Edward (1910). He also had three older children (all named Reynolds) living in the household in 1901 and 1911, Ethel, Henry and Florence. In 1911 they were recorded as 'step'-children, but they may have been children of his previous marriage.

3. John Reynolds; born about 1861–3; as he and George both stated they were thirty-eight in 1901 and forty-nine in 1911 they may have been twins. He was a druggist's assistant living in Charlemont Mall, Dublin, in 1901 and 1911. He and his wife Mary were both Church of Ireland in 1901 and 1911. Mary was stated as being married nineteen years by 1911 and having had no children born alive.

4. Lillie Reynolds; possibly the Eliza Jane baptised in Rathdrum on 14 February 1864. Connolly's widow died in 1938.

Connolly's Children

James Connolly and Lillie Reynolds had seven children:

1. Mona Elizabeth Connolly; born in Edinburgh, 11 April 1891; died in Dublin, 4 August 1904, in most tragic circumstances; buried in Glasnevin.[37]

2. Nora Margaret Connolly; born in Edinburgh, 14 November 1893;[38] a life-long socialist activist; a Senator from 1957 to 1969; married in Dublin, 6 February 1922 James ('Seamus') O'Brien; died 1981.

3. Aideen Lily Connolly; born in Edinburgh, 1895; married in Dublin, 26 November 1919, Hugh Ward.

4. Ina Mary Connolly; born in Dublin, 1896; married in Belfast, 5 June 1920, Archibald Heron, who served as a TD in 1937–8.

5. Moira Elizabeth Connolly; born in Dublin, 1 January 1899; medical doctor; married in London, 1940, Richard C. Beech.

6. Roderic James Connolly; born in Dublin, 11 February 1901; took an active part in the 1916 Easter Rising at the GPO, along with his father. He was a leading trade unionist. He served as a TD in 1943–4 and 1948–51 and as a Senator in 1973–7. He married firstly in Dublin, 30 July 1921, Jessie Ida Maidment, who died in 1930. He married secondly in Glasgow, 1937, Margaret ('Peggy') Stafford. He died in 1980.

7. Fiona A. Connolly; born in USA, 1906–7; married firstly in Dublin, 6 June 1931 Michael Deegan; married secondly in London, 1934, Leonard F. Wilson. She died in 1976.

Sean O'Sullivan RHA 34.

Seán Mac Diarmada

Seán Mac Diarmada was an important strategist in the IRB and responsible for infiltrating other nationalist organisations. In 1913 he became secretary of the IRB supreme council. He was thirty-three years old when he was executed in Kilmainham Gaol on 12 May 1916.

Mac Diarmada was born John McDermott or Dermott in 'Corranmore' in north Co. Leitrim in January 1883. Corranmore was not an official townland name but a name locally applied to an area of Cloonclare civil (and Roman Catholic) parish. The family's property actually straddled the boundary between two townlands, Laghty Barr (on the north-eastern side of Thur Mountain) and Kiltyclogher. The area is close to Leitrim's boundary with Co. Fermanagh, now the border between the Republic and Northern Ireland. Mac Diarmada's exact date of birth is uncertain. His baptism is recorded as 30 January but the civil birth record (registered on 10 April) erroneously states that he was born on 29 March.

It has been said that Mac Diarmada ran away from home aged fifteen and went to Glasgow to an uncle or cousin who worked as a gardener. However, he was still at home in Laghty

Barr at the time of the 1901 Census, when he was recorded as aged sixteen, though he was then eighteen. According to the *Dictionary of Irish Biography*, while working in Belfast he was sworn into the IRB. Later he moved to Dublin. In the 1911 Census he was recorded as Seaghán Mac Diarmada, living as a boarder at 15 Russell Place, part of the North Circular Road. Though he was twenty-eight he was recorded as aged twenty-six.

Mac Diarmada never married, but according to the *Dictionary of Irish Biography* from 1915 he was romantically attached to Mary Josephine 'Min' Ryan. She and her sisters were his last visitors prior to his execution. In 1919 Min married Richard Mulcahy, a future government minister. Her brother James Ryan also went on to become a government minister. Her sister Phyllis was the wife of Seán T. O'Kelly while he was President of Ireland. He had been married previously to her sister Mary Kate.

Seán Mac Diarmada came from a rural area of Leitrim where the older generations were bilingual. The 1901 Census shows his father Donald as speaking both Irish and English but none of the children, including John (Seán), could speak Irish. Ten years later the household return was written in Irish, with Donald and his sons Pat and James (Séamus) recorded as bilingual.

All available nineteenth-century records for the area are written in English. In them Mac Diarmada's father appears as Donald or Daniel, while the surname is as often rendered without the prefix 'Mc' as with it. Mac Diarmada's mother, Mary McMorrow, was from the adjacent townland of

Loughros, on the eastern slope of Thur Mountain. Cloonclare parish had numerous (Mc)Dermott and McMorrow (or McMorry) households, with many marriages between people of the surnames making it extremely difficult to distinguish between families. Without the Leitrim Genealogy Centre's databases on Rootsireland.ie it would not have been possible to establish the families of Mac Diarmada's mother's siblings in particular.

Mac Diarmada's Father's Background

Seán Mac Diarmada's father Donald (Mc)Dermott was born in the general area of Cloonclare about 1823–9 (based on his stated age in the census returns and at death). He was described variously as a farmer and a carpenter. His father was Patrick (Mc)Dermott, a farmer. As the surviving baptismal records of Cloonclare Roman Catholic parish date only from 1841 there is no possibility of tracing his ancestry further. Helpfully, however, the Leitrim Genealogy Centre's databases on Rootsireland.ie include civil records, which is useful particularly in relation to marriages and deaths in this family.

Patrick held a piece of land that straddled the border between Laghty Barr and Kiltyclogher townlands, an area with the alternative name of Corranmore. The house on the property was recorded in Kiltyclogher townland in Griffith's *Primary Valuation* (1857). In the late nineteenth century the townland boundaries were altered, which was an extremely unusual occurrence. In the Valuation Office revision books the house was transferred to Laghty Barr. It would appear that Patrick (Mc)Dermott died in the latter half of the nineteenth century. He may have been the Patrick Dermott of 'Cornmore', farmer, who died on 26 July 1874 at the stated age of seventy-one.[39] The informant on his death record was Honor Dermott.

The property in Laghty Barr (Lot 5) and Kiltyclogher (Lot 24) was shared from the 1870s/1880s between Daniel (Donald) and Catherine McDermott. In the 1890 revision the property was divided between them and it was then that Donald's part of the buildings was transferred to Laghty Barr while Catherine's remained in Kiltyclogher. It is very probable that Catherine was Donald's mother and that she was the Catherine McDermott of Corranmore, widow of Patrick McDermott, farmer, who died on 23 February 1895 at the stated age of eighty-eight.[40] The informant on her death record was Thomas McDermott of Corranmore. Certainly, Catherine's part of the property passed to a Thomas McDermott and eventually to Donald's grandson John James McDermott.

In the 1901 Census one of the various (Mc)Dermott households in Kiltyclogher townland was that of Thomas McDermott (born *c.*1837) and his sisters Honor (born *c.*1839) and Kate (born *c.*1855). In the 1911 Census the return for what seems to be the same household was written in Irish. Caitlín (born *c.*1837) and Aine Ni Diarmuda (born *c.*1845) were living there, while the name Domhnall Mac Diarmuda was written in but crossed through.

Mac Diarmada's Mother's Background

Seán Mac Diarmada's mother Mary McMorrow was baptised in Cloonclare parish on 15 March 1845. The baptismal register does not give addresses and, knowing only that her father was Patrick McMorrow of Loughros, it would not have been possible to identify her in the parish records were it not for her sister's application for the Old Age Pension in 1917.[41] Her sister Catherine needed proof of age (possibly because her baptism was omitted from the parish register) and applied for a search of the 1851 Census (destroyed in 1922). On the Census Search Form she stated that her parents were Pat McMorrow and Anne Rynn of Loughros. The resulting search of the census identified Patt and Anne McMorry or McMorrow. The form recorded that the census return stated that they married in 1838 and had seven children – Ellen (aged eleven), Denis (nine), Anne (seven), Mary (five), Catherine (three), Bridget (one) and Patt, who had died.

In Griffith's *Valuation* (1857) there were two McMorrows in Loughros, Patrick and Michael, with separate houses but mostly shared land. In the Tithe Applotment Book for Cloonclare parish (1834) there was one McMorrow holding, that of Denis. As Patrick McMorrow and Anne Rynn's eldest son was also Denis, it is possible to speculate that the Denis McMorrow in the Tithe Applotment was father of both Patrick and Michael McMorrow in Griffith's *Valuation*. It is *probable*, therefore, that Denis McMorrow of Loughros was Seán Mac Diarmada's great-grandfather. Denis held eight Irish acres of pasture in Loughros in 1834, but apparently he was dead by 1857. Denis would appear to have had at least two sons, Michael and Patrick. Michael disappeared from Loughros sometime in the 1860s or 1870s. Patrick was Seán Mac Diarmada's grandfather.

Patrick McMorrow was born about 1812–14 (based on his stated age in the 1901 Census and at death) and he was a farmer in Loughros into the early twentieth century, dying on 12 April 1904.[42] He married Anne Rynn (or Wren) in 1838, according to the 1851 Census. Anne was born about 1816–18 (based on her stated age in the 1901 Census and at death) and she died on 1 March 1904, a few weeks before her husband.[43] Like Mac Diarmada's father, Patrick and Anne were bilingual, according to the 1901 Census. Their sons James and Michael were not listed as speaking Irish and English in 1901 but in 1911 they were.

Patrick McMorrow and Anne Rynn (or Wren) had twelve known children:

1. Ellen McMorrow; born about 1839–40; living in 1851.
2. Denis McMorrow; born about 1841–2; married 11 July 1870 Anne Gilgun of Meenkeeragh; they lived in Kiltyclogher townland; their children were Patrick (1871), John (1872), Hugh (1873), Michael (1875), Anne (1877), Myles (1879), James (1882), Denis (1884), Joseph (1886), Thomas (1888) and Francis (1893).
3. Anne McMorrow; baptised in Cloonclare Roman Catholic parish, 23 December 1843; married 21 January 1864 Andrew McMorrow of Briscloonagh in

Cloonclare parish; their children were Ellen (1865), Mary (1867), James (1869), Patrick (1872), James (1875), Anne (1879), Andrew (1881) and Michael (1885).

4. Mary McMorrow; baptised 15 March 1845; married Donald McDermott of Corranmore and was the mother of Seán Mac Diarmada (see below).

5. Patrick McMorrow; baptised 25 March 1847; dead by the time of the 1851 Census.

6. Catherine McMorrow; born about 1848; married 19 January (civil record states 2 February) 1871 Terence McDermott (son of Malachi) of Corranmore (actually within Kiltyclogher townland); their children were Mary (1871), John (1873), Patrick (1875), Bridget (1877), Anne (1879), Terence (1881), James (1883), Catherine (1885), Margaret (1888), Lacky/Malachy (1890) and Ellen (1893).

7. Bridget McMorrow; born about 1849–50; married 14 January 1875 Thomas Flynn of Loughros Barr; their children were James (1876), John (1877), Michael (1880), Patrick (1886) and Thomas (1890).

8. James McMorrow; born about 1851–6; unmarried as of 1911; remained farming in Loughros with his brother Michael until about 1934, when they were replaced in the property by Myles Dolan.

9. Michael McMorrow; born about 1851–61; unmarried as of 1911; remained farming in Loughros with his brother James until about 1934, when they were replaced in the property by Myles Dolan.

10. Winifred McMorrow; baptised 19 May 1856; married 13 December 1877 Henry O'Brien of Gortnalibret in Cloonclare parish; their children were Mary Anne (1878), Patrick (1880), Catherine (1882), Ellen (1884), Thomas (1886) and Margaret (1889), all born in Gortnalibret.

11. Margaret McMorrow; baptised 3 December 1859; married 29 February 1892 James McMorrow of Aughavanney in Cloonclare parish; their children were Mary Anne (1894), Mary Ellen (1896), Peter (1897) and Patrick (1898).

12. Patrick McMorrow; baptised 30 December 1862.

Mac Diarmada's Immediate Family

Seán Mac Diarmada's father Donald McDermott was born about 1823–9. He worked as a farmer and a carpenter, occupying a farm in 'Corranmore' (sometimes also called Scregg) that straddled the boundary between the townlands of Laghty Barr and Kiltyclogher. In the 1901 and 1911 Censuses the family's house was returned under Laghty Barr. Donald McDermott married Mary McMorrow (McMurrough), from the adjacent townland of Loughros, on 28 February 1867 in Glenfarne Roman Catholic church. Glenfarne was then a church within Cloonclare Roman Catholic parish but it now constitutes a separate parish.

Mac Diarmada's mother Mary died on 1 March 1892, just short of her forty-seventh birthday, though her stated age was forty-five.[44] She was survived by her husband Donald who died on 19 September 1913, at the stated age of eighty-nine.[45]

Donald McDermott and Mary McMorrow had ten children:

1. Patrick McDermott; born in Corranmore, 5 April 1869; baptised in Cloonclare Roman Catholic parish, 6 April 1869. He was a farmer and he remained living in the family home in Laghty Barr. On 21 April 1902 in Kiltyclogher Roman Catholic church, he married Mary O'Hara of Corranmore. They had at least eight children, Rose (1902), Donald (1904), John James (1906), Patrick (1908), Mary Anne (1911), Kathleen (1912), Terence (1914) and Bridget (1918). Patrick was still alive in 1955 but deceased by December 1961, at which time his sons Donald, John James and Terence were living.

2. Terence McDermott; born in Corranmore, March 1871 (birth recorded as 28 March and baptism as 23 March). He was deceased by August 1944 and possibly died as a child, but no death record has been identified. He was not in the family's 1901 Census return.

3. Mary Anne McDermott; born in Corranmore, 18 October 1872; died in New York, USA, 12 December 1961. She emigrated to the USA, possibly as early as 1898. On 5 September 1909 at the Church of the Holy Spirit, Asbury Park, New Jersey, she married William Dick, a plumber. They lived in the Brooklyn

area of New York City and were resident at 566 47th Street from at least 1930 until Mary's death, William having predeceased her. They had no children.

4. Catherine McDermott; born in Scregg, April 1874 (birth recorded as 17 April and baptism as 8 April); died unmarried in New York, USA, 25 September 1955. In 1930 and 1940 she was living with Mary and William Dick at 566 47th Street, Brooklyn, New York. In 1930 she was working as a hairdresser. On her death record she was stated as a beautician.

5. Margaret McDermott; born in Scregg, December 1876 (birth recorded as 24 December and baptism as 15 December); died in Corranmore, 18 June 1966. She was living at home in Laghty Barr in 1901. On 10 February 1902 in Kiltyclogher Roman Catholic church, she married Patrick McDermott (son of Patrick) of Corranmore (Kiltyclogher townland), a farmer. They had two children, Mary Anne (1902) and Katie Bridget (1905 [later Mrs Keaney]).

6. Beezy/Bessie McDermott; born in Corranmore, February 1879 (birth recorded as 5 March and baptism as 8 February); died unmarried in New York, USA, 13 December 1943. She was a seamstress living at home in Laghty Barr in 1901. She emigrated to the USA, supposedly in 1905. After a visit home to Ireland she re-entered the USA in the company of her sister Rose, arriving in New York on 11 October 1910. In 1939 her address was 1973 South Park Avenue, Lackawanna, New York.

7. Rose MacDermott (as she spelled it); born in
    Laghty, 30 April 1881; baptised 30 April 1881; died
    unmarried in New York, USA, 15 January 1968.
    She was living at home in Laghty Barr in 1901. She
    immigrated to the USA, arriving in New York on 11
    October 1910 in the company of her sister Bessie.[46]
    In 1930 and 1940 she was living with Mary and
    William Dick at 566 47th Street, Brooklyn, New
    York, and she continued to live at that address
    into the 1960s. In 1930 she was a bookkeeper
    and in 1940 she was a secretary. She returned to
    visit Corranmore in July 1965, by which time her
    siblings in the USA were all deceased.

8. John McDermott (Seán Mac Diarmada); born in
    Corranmore, January 1883 (birth recorded as 29
    March and baptism as 30 January).

9. Donald McDermott; born in Corranmore, 4 August
    1885. He immigrated to the USA. In 1930 and
    1940 he was unmarried and living with Mary and
    William Dick at 566 47th Street, Brooklyn, New
    York. In 1930 he worked in an elevator and in 1940
    he was a waiter in a restaurant. He was still alive in
    August 1944 but deceased by December 1961.

10. James McDermott (Séamus Mac Diarmada); born
    in Corranmore, 7 December 1887; baptised 9
    December 1887. It is said that he immigrated in
    1914 to the USA, where he was active in Clan
    na Gael. It is also said that he was editor of the
    Gaelic American following the death of John Devoy

in 1928.[47] He was still alive in August 1944 but deceased by December 1961, at which time his sons James and Seán were living at 1941 51st Street, Brooklyn, New York.

Seán Mac Diarmada visited the USA once. He sailed (as John McDermott) on the 'Caledonia' from Londonderry, arriving in New York on 15 September 1912.[48] The passenger list shows that he was 5 feet 8 inches in height and had dark hair and grey eyes. Rather than naming one of his siblings as the person he was to visit he named a friend, John F. Bennett of 1041 Bedford Avenue, Brooklyn. The *Dictionary of Irish Biography* states that Mac Diarmada's visit was to attend the Clan na Gael convention in Atlantic City.

In the late 1930s Mac Diarmada's five sisters successfully claimed Military Service pensions in respect of his activities.[49] The correspondence concerning these claims provided information, including their addresses, as well as death records and, for the two married sisters, marriage records.

Seán O'Sullivan A.R.H.A 1922

Thomas MacDonagh

Thomas MacDonagh was the last of the seven signatories to be admitted to the secret council that planned the Rising. Through the Gaelic League he had come in contact with Patrick Pearse and become a staff member of Pearse's Irish language school, St Enda's. Through literary circles he developed a friendship with Joseph Plunkett, his future brother-in-law. During the Rising MacDonagh was in command of the battalion that occupied Jacob's biscuit factory (now home to the National Archives) in Bishop Street. He was thirty-eight years old when he was executed in Kilmainham Gaol on 3 May 1916.

MacDonagh was born in Cloughjordan, Co. Tipperary, on 1 February 1878, the son of two teachers. His secondary school education was in Rockwell College near Cashel, under the Holy Ghost Fathers. He later entered the congregation as a novice and joined the college staff as a teacher of languages. He was there at the time of the 1901 Census, but later that year he abandoned the thought of becoming a priest and joined the teaching staff of St Kieran's College, Kilkenny. It was in Kilkenny that he first encountered the Gaelic League and this ignited his nationalist fervour. Later he worked in St

Colman's in Fermoy before moving to Dublin and becoming more involved in the literary world. In the 1911 Census, then living alone near St Enda's in Haroldsgrange, Rathfarnham, he described himself as a poet and teacher. Later that year he was awarded an MA by the National University of Ireland.

Thomas MacDonagh's Father's Background

Thomas MacDonagh's father Joseph was born about 1834–5, according to the stated age on his death record. The *Dictionary of Irish Biography* states that he was a native of Co. Roscommon and the son of a small farmer, after whose death Thomas's mother and her brother, a parish priest, sent him to train as a teacher in Dublin. In Shane Kenna's biography of Thomas MacDonagh in the O'Brien Press *16 Lives* series, Joseph is stated as being from Kilglass on the Sligo–Roscommon border. Apparently, Joseph's first teaching job was in Cloghan in King's Co. (now Co. Offaly). It was there that in 1868 he married a fellow teacher, Mary Parker. After some years they moved to Cloughjordan. Joseph died there of influenza on 31 January 1894 at the stated age of fifty-nine.[50]

There are two places in Co. Roscommon called Kilglass and neither is near the border with Sligo. Kilglass, Co. Sligo, is also not near the border. As Joseph died before the 1901 Census there is no source in which to confirm his native county. If Kilglass was indeed where he was from, the most likely place is the Roman Catholic parish of Kilglass, on the Roscommon borders with counties Leitrim and Longford.

However, there was no McDonagh (or variants) entry in Griffith's *Primary Valuation* in Kilglass civil parish.

Unfortunately, neither the *Midland Counties Advertiser* (Roscrea) nor the *Nenagh Guardian* carried a full obituary for Joseph. This type of source would likely have thrown some light on his background. An added problem is that many Roscommon Roman Catholic parishes, including Kilglass and Ballinameen (see below), have no surviving baptismal records for the 1830s.

On his marriage record Joseph stated that his father was Patt McDonough (the spelling he also used), a farmer. As his father apparently died while Joseph was still young it is unlikely that the father was alive when Griffith's *Valuation* was published for the Roscommon area (1857–8). Therefore, it is more likely that his mother would be listed in Griffith's *Valuation*. The problem is that her name is unknown.

It is by no means a safe practice to rely on naming patterns when doing genealogical research in Ireland, but they may inform the search. Joseph MacDonagh and Mary Parker named their eldest son, Patrick, after his paternal grandfather. However, they named their second son Joseph rather than after Mary's father, Thomas. Therefore, they did not adhere strictly to the usual pattern with the boys. Their eldest daughters were named Mary and Ellen/Eleanor. It is possible that these were the names of both grandmothers, but this is pure speculation.

The female McDonagh (or variant) entries in Griffith's *Valuation* in Co. Roscommon were relatively few. Those recorded simply as 'Widow' held no land. Likewise, the only Mary held no land. There were two Eleanors, but only one of them had a farm. This was Eleanor McDonagh in Knockroe townland in Estersnow civil parish. She had about twenty-one acres, rented from Viscount Lorton. Estersnow is in the northern part of Co. Roscommon, but not on the border with Sligo. In Roman Catholic divisions it is part of Ballinameen parish, which does adjoin Sligo. The only person of the surname living in Knockroe in 1901 was Thomas McDonough, an unmarried farmer aged seventy-two. He was gone by 1911.

Unless there is further information held by the family or contained in Thomas MacDonagh's papers, it is not at all likely that his paternal line can be traced further.

MacDonagh's Mother's Background

Thomas MacDonagh's mother was Mary Parker. According to the *Dictionary of Irish Biography*, she was born in Dublin to English parents and her father had moved to Dublin to work as compositor in Greek for Trinity College Press. According to Shane Kenna, her father was a Unitarian. Based on her stated age in the 1901 Census, she was born about 1843–4.

Various sources refer to her as Mary Louise. It may be that she used the name Mary L. MacDonagh in her literary attempts. Otherwise there would appear to be no basis for believing she had a second forename. In all documentary references to her found in this investigation she was named as Mary. In any case, Louisa was the form of the name in common usage in the nineteenth century, rather than the

French version Louise. In 1907 she was successful in having a story, 'Three Tipperary Boys' published by the Catholic Truth Society of Ireland (CTSI). A copy of this has not yet been found, but an online reference to it gave her name as Mary L. MacDonagh and her maiden name as Burroughs Parker.[51] This maiden name is significant but the source for it in this instance has not been ascertained. The letter from the CTSI accepting her story addressed her simply as Mrs MacDonagh.[52]

The Parker family has proved a lot harder to trace than might have been expected. On her marriage record Mary stated that her father was Thomas Parker, a printer. The only potentially relevant baptismal reference for Mary was found in the FamilySearch.org 'Ireland Births and Baptisms, 1620–1881' database. This related to the 'birth' on 13 September 1843 of Mary daughter of Thomas Burroughs Parker in Eustace Street Presbyterian Church, Dublin. No reference to any other child of a Thomas Parker being baptised in this church is contained in the database.

In the 1840s Eustace Street was one of two Dublin congregations of the Synod of Munster, then part of the Association of Irish Non-Subscribing Presbyterians. The other was Great Strand Street. The Eustace Street and Strand Street congregations both espoused Unitarianism. Both later merged in what is now the St Stephen's Green congregation.[53] It appears that the FamilySearch.org database covers the baptismal registers of both Eustace Street and Strand Street, labelled as Eustace Street. It has been confirmed that Mary Parker's baptism was not recorded in Eustace Street so, presumably, she was baptised in Strand

Street. In any case, she appears to have been the only child of this Thomas Burroughs Parker baptised in either of the two Dublin Unitarian congregations. The facts that this child was of a Unitarian family and that the name Burroughs appears in the entry do not conclusively prove that she was the same person as MacDonagh's mother.

A general online search for Thomas Burroughs Parker revealed reference to the dissolution of a printing and stationery partnership in London in 1868. A notice in *The London Gazette* on 13 November 1868 indicated that the firm of Brown and Parker, printers and stationers, at 7a North Buildings, Eldon Street, and 7 Mark Lane was dissolved on 10 November by mutual agreement between the partners, Charles Rowland Brown and Thomas Burroughs Parker.[54]

Further references were found to Thomas Burroughs Parker. He appeared in Electoral Registers as follows: in 1868 at 16 Peak Hill Avenue, Sydenham; in 1875 at 5 Rydon Crescent, Clerkenwell (described as printer); in 1887 at 24 Archibald Road, Islington.[55]

The marriage register of St Mary, Islington, held in London Metropolitan Archives has a relevant entry on 2 January 1837. It is for Thomas Burroughs Parker and Sarah Ann Suggate, both of that parish and both previously unmarried.[56]

In the 1841 Census in White Conduit Grove, St Mary Islington West, Thomas Parker (aged twenty-eight; compositor) was living with his wife Sarah (twenty-five) and his daughter Emily (nine months). In 1851 at 38 Skinner Street, Clerkenwell, Thomas Parker (thirty-eight; printer's compositor; born in Islington) was living with his wife Sarah (thirty-five) and his children Emily (ten) and Henry (eight), both born in Islington. He was not found in 1861, but in 1871 at 5 Rydon Crescent, Clerkenwell, Thomas B. Parker (fifty-eight; printer; b. in the City) was living with his wife Sarah Ada [*sic*] (fifty-two). Finally, in 1881 at 3 Chesterfield Street, Thomas B. Parker (sixty-eight; retired printer reader) was living with his wife Sarah A. (sixty-four). The Calendar of Wills and Administrations for England and Wales for 1890 showed that Thomas Burroughs Parker of 8 Granville Terrace, Wood Green, died on 16 November 1890 and his will was proved by his son Henry Thomas Parker, teacher of music.

On the surface this Thomas Burroughs Parker, printer, living in London for much of the latter half of the nineteenth century could hardly be the father of the Mary Parker baptised in Dublin in 1843. However, the London Freedom of the City Admission Papers provided another tantalising reference. This entry showed that on 23 October 1865 Thomas Burroughs Parker of 7a North Buildings (the address of Brown and Parker, above), a printer, was admitted a freeman of London by redemption in the Company of Spectacle Makers of London. Incidentally, since 1752 it had not been a requirement to be a spectacle maker to gain admission to the company. He was stated as son of Thomas Burroughs Parker, late of Dublin, printer, deceased.[57]

Two other interesting references were found in the FamilySearch.org 'England Births and Christenings, 1538–1975' database. One referred to the baptism in St Mary Magdalene's, Old Fish Street, London, on 23 June 1811 of Richard Knight Parker, son of Thomas Burrows Parker and his wife Mary. The other was to the baptism in Lion Walk Independent meetinghouse in Colchester, Essex, on 31 August 1817 of Thomas Burroughs Parker, son of Thomas Burroughs Parker, and his wife Mary. The child's date of birth was 28 February 1813.

There is scope for much further research on this family to determine whether it is, in fact, that of Thomas MacDonagh's mother. For now only an outline of its *possible* history can be given. Thomas Burroughs Parker, a printer, and his wife Mary apparently lived in London in the early 1810s, where their sons Richard Knight (1811) and Thomas Burroughs (1813) were born. By 1817 they were in Colchester, where their younger son was baptised in the Non-Conformist Lion Walk meetinghouse. At some point they must have lived in Dublin and by 1865 Thomas Burroughs Parker, Senior, was deceased. Thomas Burroughs Parker, Junior, was also in the printing trade. In 1837 he married Sarah Ann Suggate in Islington, where their children Emily Ann (1840)[58] and Henry Thomas (1842)[59] were born. The family moved to Dublin, where another child, Mary, was born in 1843 and baptised in Strand Street Presbyterian church on 13 September 1843. They had returned to London by 1851.

The main problem with this narrative is that Mary was not living with the family in London in 1851. It is possible that she remained in Dublin with her grandparents or indeed that the family's term of residence in London at that time was only brief. They were not found in London in 1861 and the next mention of Thomas Burroughs Parker, Junior, was when he was admitted a freeman of London in 1865.

If Mary MacDonagh was the child baptised in 1843 and if she was the daughter of Thomas Burroughs Parker and Sarah Ann Suggate, then Thomas MacDonagh was the nephew of a fairly distinguished composer and conductor, Henry Parker, who died in 1917.

MacDonagh's Immediate Family

Thomas MacDonagh's father Joseph MacDonagh was born about 1834–5. He worked as a teacher in Cloghan in King's Co. He married Mary Parker, also a teacher, on 20 February 1868 in Cloghan Roman Catholic chapel in Banagher (otherwise Gallen & Reynagh) Roman Catholic parish. In the latter half of the 1870s they moved to Cloughjordan, Co. Tipperary. Joseph died on 31 January 1894. Mary died in 1908.

Joseph MacDonagh and Mary Parker had nine known children:

1. Patrick MacDonagh; baptised in Banagher Roman Catholic parish, 31 October 1869; died of convulsions in Cloghan, 18 December 1869.
2. Mary MacDonagh; baptised in Banagher, 12 March 1871. She entered the Religious Sisters of Charity and was in their convent in Basin Lane, Dublin, in 1911.
3. Joseph MacDonagh; baptised in Banagher, 25 July 1873; died of typhus fever in Cloughjordan, 28 February 1881.

4. Ellen (or Eleanor Louisa) MacDonagh; born in Cloghan, 24 June 1875; married in Cloughjordan, 8 September 1897, Daniel Bingham of Ballina, Co. Tipperary, Acting Sergeant of the Royal Irish Constabulary at Newport, Co. Tipperary. In 1901 Eleanor Louisa was living in Ballina. By 1911 Daniel was clerk of Petty Sessions and the family was living in Broadford, Co. Clare. By that time they had six children but only four were still living. Their known children were George Joseph (1898), Herbert John (1900), Henry (1902; dead by 1911), Arthur James (1904) and Aileen Mary (1910).

5. Thomas MacDonagh; born in Cloughjordan, 1 February 1878.

6. John MacDonagh; born in Cloughjordan, 4 October 1879; he took part in the 1916 Rising, alongside his brother Thomas in Jacob's factory, and later received a Military Service pension; John was a film maker and playwright; in later life he lived in Goatstown, Co. Dublin; he married in 1925 Eileen Philippa Coyne; he died 1 July 1961; his wife died on 30 January 1984; they had no surviving children.[60]

7. James MacDonagh; born and baptised in Cloughjordan, 8 May 1881; an orchestral musician in England; married 1903 Evangeline (Eva) Lauraine; children Jessie (1903), Terence (1908), Brian (1910) and Muriel (1916). His son Terence was a well-known musician, playing the oboe and cor anglais.

8. Joseph Michael MacDonagh; born and baptised in Cloughjordan, 18 May 1883; elected an MP for Tipperary North in 1918 and was part of the first Dáil Éireann; in the Civil War he took the Anti-Treaty side. He died in Mountjoy Gaol in 1922. His daughter Mary (Moll) was born in 1913 and married in 1937 in Dublin Francis (Frank) Lemass.

9. Elizabeth MacDonagh; born in Cloughjordan, 27 May 1886; baptised in Cloughjordan, 28 May 1886; died of bronchitis in Cloughjordan, 10 January 1887.

MacDonagh's Wife and Children

MacDonagh's wife was Muriel Enid Gifford, daughter of Frederick Gifford, a Roman Catholic solicitor, and his wife Isabella Julia Burton, a member of the Church of Ireland. Muriel was born in Dublin in 1885. She and all her siblings were raised as Church of Ireland. On 3 January 1912 she married Thomas MacDonagh. Muriel's younger sister Grace Eveline (born 1888) famously married Joseph Mary Plunkett in Kilmainham Gaol on the eve of his execution. The Plunkett marriage took place on the day MacDonagh was executed. A year after the Easter Rising, in July 1917, Muriel drowned while swimming at Skerries.

Thomas MacDonagh and Muriel Gifford had two children:

1. Donnchad (Donagh) MacDonagh; born 22 November 1912; writer and judge; married firstly

in Dublin, 1935, Maura Smyth; married secondly in Dublin, 1943, Nuala Smyth, his first wife's sister. He had two children by Maura and two by Nuala. Donagh MacDonagh died on 1 January 1968.

2. Barbara MacDonagh; born March 1915; married in Dublin, 1936 William Gerard (Liam) Redmond, a well-known actor. They had four children.

Graham Sutherland 1936

Patrick Pearse

Patrick Pearse is seen as the key figure in the Easter Rising. As the leader of the Irish Volunteers who took part in the rebellion, he was in a commanding position. He had a complex personality and in the century since 1916 his character has been studied more than those of the other six signatories. He was thirty-six years old when he was executed in Kilmainham Gaol on 3 May 1916.

Patrick Henry Pearse was born on 10 November 1879 at 27 Great Brunswick Street (now Pearse Street), Dublin. His father, James Pearse, was an English stonemason and monumental sculptor who came to Dublin in the early 1860s. James's second wife, Margaret Brady, was the mother of Patrick and his younger brother Willie, another participant in the Rising. Patrick graduated from the Royal University of Ireland in 1900 and was called to the bar in 1901. He founded St Enda's School in 1908 in Ranelagh and it later transferred to the Hermitage, above Rathfarnham.

Pearse's Paternal Line

Pearse's paternal grandfather was James Pearse, a picture-frame maker or composition maker, who was born in London in the late 1810s. His stated age in census returns suggested a date of birth varying from 1817 to 1821, but he married in 1837. In the 1861 Census he gave his birthplace as Bloomsbury, the area in which his sons were born. It is possible that he was the James, son of William and Ann Pearce, baptised on 1 June 1817 in St Giles in the Fields parish. The address on the baptismal record was 8 Queen Street, Seven Dials, and the father was a tailor.[61] Queen Street is now called Shorts Gardens. It is south of St Giles in the Fields and of what is now considered Bloomsbury.

James married Mary Ann Thompson in St Martin's in the Fields church, London, on 12 March 1837, months before the introduction of civil registration.[62] Mary Ann was born in London and she was a few years older than her husband, with her stated age suggesting a birth date about 1811–16. They lived for the first few years of their marriage at 24 Plumtree Street in the Bloomsbury area of London, where their three sons were born. By 1851 they had moved to Birmingham, where they were living in Ellis Street. In 1861 they were just around the corner in Gough Street.

According to Róisín Ní Ghairbhí's biography of Willie Pearse in the O'Brien Press *16 Lives* series, Patrick and Willie's grandmother died in 1875.[63] The Index of Deaths for England and Wales contains an entry for a Mary Ann Pearse, aged sixty-one, in Birmingham in 1875. It would appear that James Pearse remarried after his wife's death. In the 1881 Census James Pearse, a gilt-picture frame maker and decorator, aged sixty-two and born in London, was living with his wife [Flamut?]al, a tailoress aged forty-six and born in Birmingham.

They were living in Bell Barn Road, Birmingham, and also in their household was Charles H. Bale, aged nine, an 'adopted' son. James visited his son in Dublin when his grandson Willie was very young, so apparently in the 1880s.[64]

James Pearse and Mary Ann Thompson had three known children:

1. William Pearse; baptised in St Giles in the Fields parish, 26 December 1837, with the family's address as 24 Plumtree Street.[65] He was a gun finisher by trade. He married firstly in St Peter's church, Birmingham, on 26 December 1859, Laura Smith, daughter of Samuel Smith, a barber.[66] Laura died in 1866.[67] William married secondly in the same church on 11 June 1867, Ann Gummery, a widow aged thirty-nine, daughter of William Birch.[68] By his first wife he had two known children, Mary J. (1860) and William (born about 1863–4). By his second wife he also had two known children, Kate (about 1867–8) and Florence M. (about 1868–9); his second wife also had children by her previous husband.

2. James Pearse; baptised in St Giles in the Fields, 29 December 1839, with address as 24 Plumtree Street;[69] father of Patrick Pearse (see below).

3. Henry Pearse; baptised in St Giles in the Fields, 11 April 1841, with address as 24 Plumtree Street.[70] He followed in his father's trade as a picture-frame maker and lived in Gough Street, Birmingham. He married in St Philip's church, Birmingham, on 29

March 1863, Sarah Ann Orchard, daughter of John
Orchard, a jeweller.[71] He had seven known children,
Arthur James (1866), Alfred Henry (1868), Kate
Elizabeth (1871), Wallace William (1872), Blanche
(1875), Harry (about 1877–8) and Thomas (about
1879–80). The eldest son, Arthur James, married
in the late 1880s and lived next door to his father
in Gough Street in 1891. Arthur's son Harry (born
about 1893) served in the Royal Warwickshire
Regiment on the Western Front during the Great
War and was killed on 26 September 1916. Arthur
felt betrayed by his Irish first cousins' involvement
in the Easter Rising. He was still alive when, in the
1960s, the BBC considered making a programme
about Patrick and Willie Pearse, and he ordered that
family papers connected with the rebel cousins be
destroyed.[72]

Pearse's Father's First Marriage

James, the second son of James Pearse and Mary Ann
Thompson, was a monumental sculptor. According to the
online *Dictionary of Irish Architects 1720–1940* (www.dia.ie),
he was brought to Dublin about 1860 by Charles William
Harrison, who came to Ireland in 1859. He was foreman
at Harrison's monumental sculpture workshop at 178 Great
Brunswick Street (later to become Pearse Street).[73] James may
not have moved permanently to Dublin at that time, as he
was listed in the 1861 Census in his father's household in

Gough Street, Birmingham, described as a stone carver. He married in St Thomas's parish church, Birmingham, on 28 April 1863, Susan Emily Fox. On the marriage record he was described as a sculptor living in St Thomas's parish. She was stated as aged 18 and living in St Martin's parish. Her father was William Fox, a chandelier maker.[74]

James and Susan Emily (or Emily Susannah, but usually recorded as Emily) were living in Dublin by December 1864, when their eldest known child was born there. They lived in the Portobello area for the first few years and in the early 1870s at 1 Wharton Terrace, Harold's Cross. When Emily died at the stated age of 30 on 26 July 1876 they were living in Great Clarence Street (now Macken Street). She was buried in Glasnevin with her two daughters who died in 1872.[75] Sometime about 1869 James, Emily and their two eldest children were received into the Roman Catholic faith at Mount Argus Passionist monastery in Harold's Cross by Rev. Pius Devine. In December 1877 the priest wrote a statement to that effect, saying that it occurred 'about 7 or 8 years ago'.[76]

In the early 1870s James began a business with Patrick J. O'Neill and their premises in the mid-1870s was 182 Great Brunswick Street. The partnership was dissolved about 1875 and James eventually based his business at 27 Great Brunswick Street, where it remained until after his death. For about a decade he was in partnership with Edmund Sharp but from 1888 James Pearse ran the business alone.[77] While visiting his brother in Birmingham, James died unexpectedly on 5 September 1900. Administration of his estate (valued at £1,470-17-6) was granted in March 1901 to his son Patrick.[78]

James Pearse and Emily Fox had four known children:

1. Mary Emily (or Emily Mary) Pearse; born in Pleasant View,[79] Portobello, 31 December 1864; baptised in St Peter's C. of I. parish, 24 January 1865. After being abandoned by her husband she worked as a qualified midwife and lived for a time in the Fanad area of Co. Donegal. She married in St Andrew's Roman Catholic parish, 5 July 1884, Alfred McGloughlin, the son of John McGloughlin, a neighbour in Great Brunswick Street who was an art metal worker. Alfred was an architect. In about 1899 he left the family following a scandal involving a servant. He went to New York and had some success in architecture.[80] Apparently he obtained a divorce, as in 1910 he was living with his Irish-born wife of three years, Annie.

   Emily Pearse and Alfred McGloughlin had three known children:

   i.   Emily Mary McGloughlin; baptised in St Michan's Roman Catholic parish, 13 July 1885.
   ii. Margaret Mary McGloughlin; baptised in St Michan's, 9 August 1886; married 1909 James McGarvey.[81] In 1911 she was living in Carrowkeel Glebe townland, Co. Donegal, with her mother and her husband. At that time she had no children.

    iii. Alfred Vincent McGloughlin; born in Dublin, in 1888. He was a draughtsman in the firm of J. & G. McGloughlin from about 1906. In 1911 he was living at the Hermitage with the Pearses. He served with the Irish Volunteers and the IRB from 1913 and he was involved in the Howth gun-running but did not take part in the Easter Rising due to illness. After the War of Independence he took the Anti-Treaty side, and his death on 5 August 1932 was deemed attributable to harsh treatment during imprisonment in the Post-Treaty period.[82] He married in Dublin, in 1914, Marcella Frances Dowling. They had seven children, James Alfred, Pearse Finbar, Fergus, Michael, Alfred (Alf MacLochlainn, author and former Director of the National Library), Charlotte Mary and John. Marcella successfully claimed a Military Service pension in respect of his activities and the file contains the details relating to their children.[83]

2. James Vincent Pearse; born in Bloomfield Place,[84] 19 December 1866; baptised in St Peter's C. of I. parish, 8 January 1867. Like his father, he was a sculptor/stone carver and he worked in the family business. He married Mary McCasey about 1886–7. It is possible that after his father's unexpected death in 1900 James's status in the business was reduced to that of employee by the influence of his

step-mother. In 1910 the business was sold and the proceeds helped obtain a lease of the Hermitage to which Patrick Pearse transferred St Enda's School.[85] In 1901 James, Mary and their family were living in relative comfort at 16 Spencer Street, near North Strand Road. In 1911 they were occupying part of a tenement building at 16 Verschoyle Place, off Mount Street. James died aged forty-five on 25 March 1912 and was buried in the family plot in Glasnevin.

James Pearse and Mary McCasey had eight children:

i.   Emily Mary Pearse; born in 1888; died 26 July 1906 and was buried in the family plot in Glasnevin.

ii.   Florence Mary Pearse; born in 1890; married in Dublin, 17 December 1915, William Scarlett. He served in the British Army during the Great War.[86] Their daughter Agnes died aged eleven months on 2 February 1918 and was buried in the Pearse family plot in Glasnevin. Their son Noel was interviewed in 2014 by Róisín Ní Ghairbhí.[87]

iii. James Vincent Pearse; born in 1892; he served in the British Army during the Great War.[88]

iv.   Agnes Pearse; born in 1894.

v.   Margaret Pearse; born about 1896–7; died unmarried, 20 May 1921, at the stated age of twenty-four; buried in the family plot in Glasnevin.

vi.   Henry Albert Pearse; born in 1899.

vii. William Pearse; born about 1901–2.

viii. Thomas Ernest Pearse; born in 1907; apparently the Thomas Ernest Pearse who married Nellie Byrne in 1933.[89]

3. Agnes Maud Pearse; born 30 November 1869; baptised in Rathmines Roman Catholic parish, 16 January 1870; died 20 October 1872 and was the first buried in the family plot in Glasnevin.

4. Agnes Kathleen (later called Amy) Pearse; born 18 June 1871; baptised (as Catharina A. Pierce) in Rathmines Roman Catholic parish, 16 July 1871; died 19 November 1872 and buried in the family plot in Glasnevin.

Pearse's Father's Second Marriage

James Pearse's first wife died in July 1876. Just over a year later he married a second time. For a widowed man left with young children there was nothing extraordinary at the time about re-marrying even within a year of his wife's death. For purely practical reasons he needed someone to help raise the children. James Pearse married Margaret Brady in St Agatha's Roman Catholic parish on 24 October 1877. The church record of the marriage shows that she was living at 7 Aldborough Avenue and that her parents were Patrick Brady and Bridget Savage. James was living at 5 Parnell Place in Harold's Cross, as was his witness, John McGloughlin. By the time their first child was born the following year, James and Margaret were living at 27 Great Brunswick Street. This remained the place of business until 1910, but in the mid-1880s the family went to live in Sandymount. They lived in a number of locations in Sandymount. Eventually a house called the Hermitage, above Rathfarnham, became the home of Patrick Pearse's St Enda's School and the family moved there.

In the 1911 Census Margaret Pearse was recorded in two locations and in two languages. She was shown as Margaret Pearse (aged fifty-four; matron of college), living with her daughter Mary Brigid (twenty-six), as paying guests in the house of Emilie Martyn in Rathfarnham village.[90] At the same time she was shown as Mairghréad Nic Phiarais (fifty-one) living in Haroldsgrange (the location of the Hermitage), with her son Pádraic Mac Piarais (thirty-one) as head of household. Also living there were her children Mairghréad (Margaret) and Uilliam (Willie), as well as her step-grandson Úilfrid Mac Lochlainn (Alfred McGloughlin) and Mairghréad Ní Bhradaigh (forty; cousin to head of household).[91] Margaret Pearse, the mother of Patrick and Willie, died in 1932, having served as a TD for Dublin County in 1921–2.

James Pearse had a further four children by Margaret Brady:

5. Margaret Mary Pearse; born at 27 Great Brunswick Street, 4 August 1878; supported her brothers' political views; remained living at St Enda's; served as TD for Dublin County in 1933–7 and was a member of the Senate from 1938 till her death; died 7 November 1968.
6. Patrick Henry Pearse; born at 27 Great Brunswick Street, 10 November 1879.

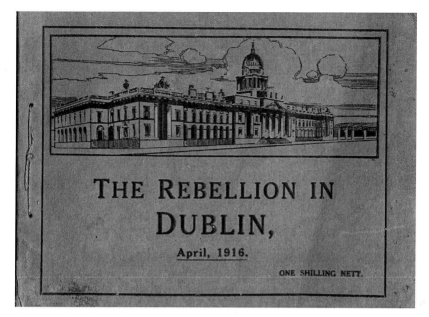

Souvenir booklet, *The Rebellion in Dublin*. All images courtesy of Kildare Library Services.

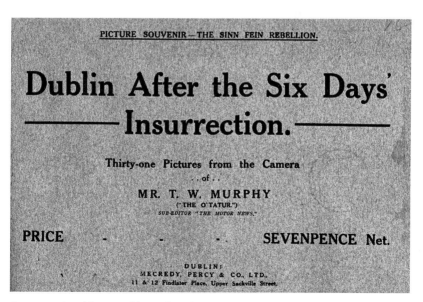

Souvenir booklet, *Dublin After the Six Days' Insurrection*.

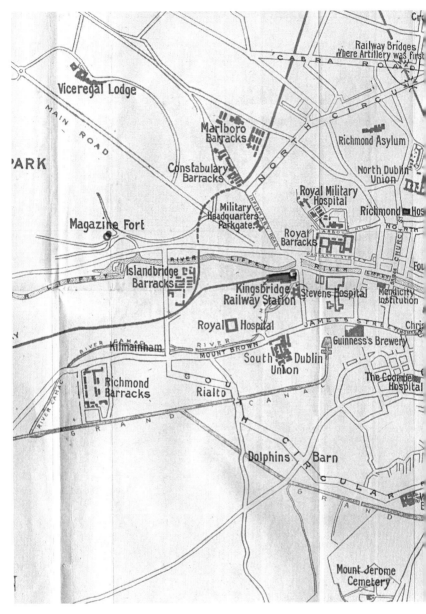

Map of Dublin in 1916 from *Sinn Fein Rebellion Handbook*.

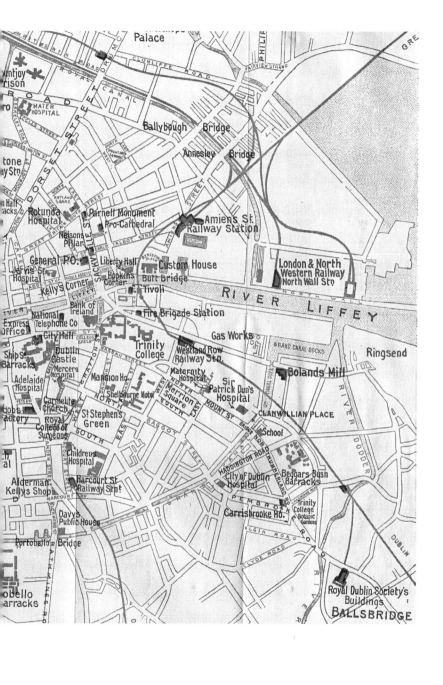

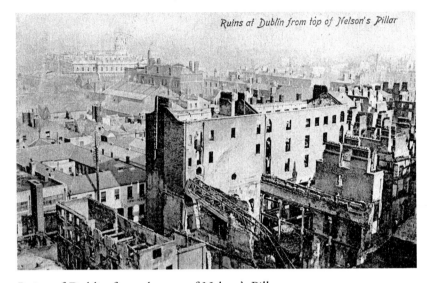

Ruins of Dublin from the top of Nelson's Pillar.

After the insurrection: Linenhall Barracks, Dublin.

Liberty Hall, Dublin, the Rebel HQ after the storming.

Joseph Plunkett. Postcard.
Dublin: Powell Press, 1916.

PUNISHMENT OF THE REBELS.

FIFTEEN MEN EXECUTED.

SIR JOHN MAXWELL'S STATEMENT.

The following announcement was issued at the Irish Headquarters Command on Thursday, 11th May :—

In view of the gravity of the rebellion and its connection with German intrigue and propaganda, and in view of the great loss of life and destruction of property resulting therefrom, the General Officer Commanding-in-Chief has found it imperative to inflict the most severe sentences on the known organisers of this detestable rising and on those Commanders who took an active part in the actual fighting which occurred. It is hoped that these examples will be sufficient to act as a deterrent to intriguers, and to bring home to them that the murder of His Majesty's liege subjects, or other acts calculated to imperil the safety of the Realm will not be tolerated.

THE PRIME MINISTER'S STATEMENT.

With the execution on Friday, 12th May, of James Connolly and John McDermott, the last of the seven men who signed the declaration of the Irish Republic on Easter Monday paid the death penalty. In the House of Commons the previous night Mr. Dillon made a remarkable speech, in which he demanded the cessation of the executions, but the Prime Minister, while expressing the hope that it would not be necessary to carry out the full punishment in many other cases, said there were two men who would have to endure the extreme penalty. The following morning it was announced that Connolly and McDermott had been executed.

The total number of rebels executed was fifteen. They were :—

P. H. Pearse.

Thomas MacDonagh.	Thos. J. Clarke.
Joseph Plunkett.	Jas. Connolly.
Edmund Kent.	John McDermott.

The above were the seven men who signed the declaration. The others who were executed for taking a prominent part in the rebellion were :—

Edward Daly.	Michael O'Hanrahan.
Wm. Pearse.	John McBride.
Cornelius Colbert.	Michael Mallin.
J. J. Heuston.	

For the murder of Head Constable Rowe at Fermoy on 2nd May

Thomas Kent

was executed on 9th May at Cork.

Sinn Fein Rebellion Handbook: 'Punishment of the rebels'.

Thomas MacDonagh, Thomas Clarke and John McBride (from souvenir booklet *The Rebellion in Dublin*).

Patrick Pearse and James Connolly (from souvenir booklet *The Rebellion in Dublin*).

Holding a Dublin street against the rebels.

Sinn Féin rebellion, 1916, O'Connell (Sackville) Street, Dublin.

7. William James (Willie) Pearse; born at 27 Great Brunswick Street, 15 November 1881; sculptor, artist and teacher; played a relatively minor role in the Easter Rising; executed in Kilmainham Gaol 4 May 1916.

8. Mary Brigid Pearse; born in Newbridge Avenue, Sandymount, 29 September 1888; did not share her brothers' republican views; later lived at 6 Beaufort Villas, Rathfarnham; died 13 November 1947.

Pearse's Maternal Line

Pearse's mother, Margaret Brady, was born in Dublin in 1857 to Patrick Brady and Bridget Savage. According to Róisín Ní Ghairbhí's biography of Willie Pearse, it was stated by Patrick Pearse that Margaret's father came to Dublin from Nobber, Co. Meath, during The Famine, along with his siblings and his father, Walter. Pearse also stated that his great-great-grandfather was Walter Brady who fought in the 1798 Rebellion and whose brother was hanged for his participation, while another was buried in the Croppies' Grave at Tara. This Walter was stated as the father of the Walter Brady who migrated to Dublin with his children at the time of The Famine. Pearse also stated that his mother's maternal uncle, James Savage, had fought in the American Civil War.[92] Róisín Ní Ghairbhí also mentioned Margaret Brady's uncle Christy Brady and his wife who had a farm outside Dublin, and her aunt Margaret who died when Willie was in his teens and who spoke Irish and told stories of rebellion.[93]

There seems to be a discrepancy in the information supplied by Pearse himself. Had his Brady ancestors lived in Nobber before moving to Dublin there should have been some trace of them in the area. The baptismal records of Nobber Roman Catholic parish go back to the eighteenth century. However, the Meath Heritage Centre's database on Rootsireland.ie shows no reference to children of a Walter (under any form of the name) Brady in Nobber parish in the period 1770–1840. In fact, the only children of a Walter Brady in the database for that period throughout the county were four children of Walter Brady and Margaret Connor baptised between 1822 and 1833. The first was Laurence, baptised in Ratoath Roman Catholic parish on 7 August 1822. The others were baptised in the adjacent Catholic parish of Curraha. They were Christopher (15 April 1827), Margaret (11 February 1831) and John (14 June 1833). No reference to the marriage of Walter Brady and Margaret Connor appeared in the Meath Heritage Centre's database or in that of Swords Historical Society, covering the neighbouring North Co. Dublin.

All the names of this family fit with those of Patrick Pearse's grandfather, Patrick Brady. In the course of this examination it has been confirmed that Patrick Brady's parents were named Walter and Margaret, and that he had siblings named Laurence, Christopher, Margaret and John. The one person missing from this Ratoath/Curraha family is Patrick himself. There is a noticeable gap in the baptisms between Laurence and Christopher and there could well have been children born before Laurence or between Christopher and Margaret. The surviving records for Ratoath and Curraha Roman Catholic parishes apparently cover the entire 1820s, but they would need to be closely examined to determine whether there are any slight gaps. In any case, there is good reason to believe that Walter Brady and Margaret Connor of Ratoath/Curraha were Patrick Pearse's great-grandparents. It is worth noting too that Tara (where a 1798 rebel Brady was supposedly buried) is much closer to Ratoath and Curraha than to Nobber.

It should be pointed out that the name Walter Brady was relatively distinctive. In Griffith's *Primary Valuation* only five individuals of that name were recorded in the entire country.[94] One was in Killeagh civil parish in north-west Co. Meath, occupying a house and garden. One was in Co. Cavan, one in Co. Westmeath, and the other two were in Dublin. These two Dublin references are significant. One was in Coolquoy Common in Kilsallaghan civil parish (published in 1847 & 1848). The property consisted of a house, office and half an acre of garden, valued at £2-11-0. This place is adjacent to the Ratoath/Curraha area of Co. Meath. The other was in the city (published in 1854). It was a property at 56 North Strand, at the junction with (North) William Street, and consisted of a house, shed and yard, valued at £10. This was certainly a property occupied by Pearse's great-grandfather.

If the Walter Brady in Coolquoy Common in Kilsallaghan civil parish in 1847–8 was the man previously living in Ratoath/Curraha he may have had younger children born at this new location. Unfortunately, the surviving records of the corresponding Roman Catholic parish of Rolestown date only from 1857. The Coolquoy Common property may have been the 'farm' outside Dublin that Christy Brady later held.

The following is what is known about Pearse's Brady ancestry from actual records.

Walter Brady was born about 1786, according to his stated age at death. His earliest known address in Dublin was 56 North Strand, at the junction with William Street. He was listed there in Griffith's *Valuation* (1854). This was the family's address when his wife Margaret (possible maiden name Connor) died on 7 January 1855 at the stated age of sixty-six (born about 1788). She was the first family member buried in Glasnevin.[95] Walter died on 9 January 1871 at the stated age of eighty-four and was buried in the same grave. On the burial record his occupation was car owner and his address was 5 King's Lane (Avenue), off Ballybough Road. However, a death announcement stated that he died at Spring Gardens, a street parallel to King's Avenue.[96]

Walter and Margaret Brady had five known children:

1. Patrick Brady; born about 1821–2, according to his stated age at death. He married Bridget Savage and it would appear that their eldest child was born before they moved to Dublin City, in or just before 1855. They were living at 56 North Strand (apparently with his parents) in 1855. In 1857–60 their address was 1 (North) Clarence Street, on the junction with North Strand. This junction no longer exists. From at least 1877 to 1894 their address was 7 Aldborough

Avenue. This cul-de-sac off Portland Row ran parallel
to North Strand. Bridget died on 22 December
1888 at the stated age of fifty-seven. She was buried
in Glasnevin in a new plot apparently adjoining
the family grave, and described as a carrier's wife.[97]
Patrick died at the Mater Hospital, 27 September
1894, and was buried with his wife. His will was
proved on 20 October 1894 by James and Margaret
Pearse. He was described as a cab proprietor and his
estate amounted to £216-14-6.[98] Patrick Brady and
Bridget Savage had four known children:

i.   Catherine Brady; born about 1852; married in
     St Agatha's Roman Catholic parish, 14 June
     1880, John Kelly, son of Patrick and Bridget
     Kelly of Greggs Lane. Up to the mid-1880s they
     lived in Clarence Street. They died young (she on
     28 January 1888 at the stated age of thirty-five)
     and their orphaned children Mary Kate and John
     lived with the Pearses for a time.[99] Catherine and
     John had four children:

     a.   Mary Catherine (Mary Kate) Kelly; baptised
          in St Agatha's, 6 May 1881; married Sydney
          Shovelton and her son, Patrick Shovelton
          (1919–2012), was a senior civil servant and
          transport executive in the UK.[100]

     b.   Patrick Kelly; baptised in St Agatha's, 27
          October 1882.

     c.   Bridget Kelly; baptised in St Agatha's, 2 May
          1884.

      d.   John Kelly; baptised in St Agatha's, 12 February 1886; killed in a traffic accident in Sandymount, 14 November 1902.[101]

  ii.   Walter Brady; born 23 March 1855; baptised in St Agatha's, 2 April 1855; died 6 April 1855, aged one week, and buried in Glasnevin with his grandmother.

 iii.   Margaret Brady; born 12 February 1857; baptised in St Agatha's, 16 February 1857; mother of Patrick Pearse (see above).

 iv.   Bridget Brady; born 15 November 1859; baptised in St Agatha's, 18 November 1859; died 7 January 1860, aged one month, and buried in Glasnevin with her brother and grandmother.

2.   Laurence Brady; possibly the Laurence baptised in Ratoath Roman Catholic parish, 7 August 1822. He married in St Agatha's Roman Catholic parish, 25 August 1861, Julia Whelan, daughter of Simon and Jane Whelan of Jervis Street. At that time his address was 4 King's Lane. He died on 17 February 1871 at the stated age of forty-five and was buried in Glasnevin.

3.   Christopher Brady; possibly the Christopher baptised in Curraha Roman Catholic parish, 15 April 1827; the granduncle Christy mentioned as having a farm with his wife outside Dublin. He married in St Mary's (Pro Cathedral) parish, 19 November 1861, Anne Keogh, daughter of William and Emily Keogh of Preban, Co. Wicklow. At that time his address was 4 King's Lane. He died on 1 July 1899 at the stated

age of sixty-five (born about 1833–4), described as a dairy owner living at 7 King's Avenue, and was buried in Glasnevin with his parents. His widow Anne died on 10 July 1902 at the stated age of sixty-eight and was buried in the same grave.

4. Margaret Brady; possibly the Margaret baptised in Curraha parish, 11 February 1831; the grandaunt mentioned as having spoken Irish and told stories of rebellion. She died on 8 May 1892 at the stated age of fifty-eight and was buried in Glasnevin.

5. John Brady; possibly the John baptised in Curraha parish, 14 June 1833. He married in St Agatha's Roman Catholic parish, 2 July 1863, Jane Fox, daughter of John and Elizabeth Fox of Kilbride, Co. Westmeath.[102] At that time his address was 4 King's Lane. John Brady was recorded as a dairy man on his daughter Margaret's birth record. He died on 2 March 1872 at the stated age of thirty-five and was buried in Glasnevin. He and Jane Fox had two known children:

    i. Margaret Mary Brady; born at 4 King's Lane, 8 January 1869;[103] she was living with the Pearse family at the Hermitage (St Enda's) in 1911; she died unmarried and aged eighty, 21 November 1949, at which time her address was St Enda's, Rathfarnham, and she was buried in Glasnevin, in the family grave with her grandparents.

    ii. Mary Jane Brady; baptised in St Agatha's Roman Catholic parish, 3 March 1871.

Pearse's Maternal Grandmother

Patrick Pearse's maternal grandparents were Patrick Brady and Bridget Savage. In the course of this investigation no record of their marriage was found. The *Dictionary of Irish Biography* entry for their daughter Margaret Pearse states that Brigid (Bridget) Savage was from Oldtown, Co. Dublin. There are four such places, in the civil parishes of Artaine, Clonmethan, Coolock and Swords. Clonmethan adjoins Kilsallaghan, where a Walter Brady was listed in Griffith's *Valuation*. Clonmethan and Kilsallaghan are two of the four civil parishes covered by Rolestown Roman Catholic parish. The only Savage entry in Griffith's *Valuation* in any of the four civil parishes covered by Rolestown RC parish was in Clonmethan, and specifically in Oldtown townland (published in 1847 & 1848). There, James Savage held a house and nine perches of garden, valued at £1-12-0. This would appear to have been adjacent to the RC chapel in the village of Oldtown.

As already mentioned, the surviving records of Rolestown Roman Catholic parish date only from 1857. If Bridget Savage was indeed from this Oldtown, it would explain why no record of her marriage to Patrick Brady was found. There is scope for further investigation of the Brady and Savage families.

Joseph Plunkett

At twenty-eight years of age, Joseph Plunkett was the youngest of the seven signatories. He was from a very different ideology and background to the other six. He favoured an independent Irish kingdom, his father was a papal count and the family was wealthy. Plunkett's marriage to Grace Gifford in Kilmainham Gaol on 3 May 1916 became an important part of the story of the Easter Rising. News of the poignant event and his execution the following day drew sympathy for the rebels from the largely hostile Irish public.

Joseph Mary Plunkett was born on 27 November 1887 at 26 Fitzwilliam Street Upper, Dublin. His father, George Noble Plunkett, had been created Count Plunkett by Pope Leo XIII in 1884, when he was just thirty-two years old. His mother was Mary Josephine (otherwise Josephine Mary) Cranny. Both Joseph's parents came from prosperous backgrounds. Their mothers were related to one another and there was a friendship between the two families. Much is known about Plunkett's background, and about Grace Gifford's family, but some accepted 'facts' about Plunkett's grandparents are inaccurate and there is scope for interesting research on most of his ancestral lines.

Plunkett's Paternal Line

All in the Blood, the memoir of Joseph's sister Geraldine, edited by her granddaughter Honor O Brolchain, preserves a large amount of oral tradition about the Plunketts and the Crannys.[104] It was the source of some of the information in the *Dictionary of Irish Biography*'s entry on Joseph Plunkett and in Honor O Brolchain's biography of Joseph in the *16 Lives* series. Geraldine Plunkett's memoir includes some interesting information that will not be found elsewhere, and which explains some apparent discrepancies in the written records. Of course, oral tradition cannot be accepted as proof on its own, and there are a few items in the memoir which do not stand up to examination.

All in the Blood states that Joseph's paternal grandfather, Patrick Joseph Plunkett, was born on a farm adjoining the demesne wall of Killeen Castle, Co. Meath. This was told to Geraldine by her grandfather himself. She added that his father was Walter Plunkett who died in 1844 and was buried 'at the foot of the Fingall vault in Killeen where his father George (1750–1824) also lay'. When The Famine came in the latter half of the 1840s Patrick and his twelve brothers and one sister abandoned the farm and the family 'scattered to other parts of Ireland and to England, but most of them, including Pat's sister, went to America'. Patrick himself went to Dublin, where he met and married Elizabeth Noble.

Geraldine added that a male ancestor of Patrick's had married an O'Daly of 'O'Daly's Bridge in Virginia, County Cavan' and that she remembered Jemima and Bedelia O'Daly of this family as old ladies who often visited her family. Their brother Willie had worked in Mexico, where he was killed by bandits, and Jemima had gone there and brought his sons back to Ireland. There is a definite flaw in Geraldine Plunkett's story. Perhaps she misinterpreted her grandfather's words or perhaps she mixed them in with information from another source. In any case it is almost certain that Patrick Plunkett was not born in the Killeen area. If he lived there at all it may have been in his later childhood.

Geraldine's information about the burials at Killeen may have its origin in a footnote to the entry on Plunket, Lords (or Earls) of Fingall in John O'Hart's *Irish Pedigrees*, Vol. 1 (fourth edition, 1887, pp. 247–8). O'Hart stated that the Fingall Plunket(t) burial place was at Killeen Castle and that 'none but members of the family who have a right of burial there are permitted to be interred'. He stated that a George Plunket, 'in the sixth degree removed in relationship to the grandfather of the present Earl [living in 1887]' was buried there in 1824 and that 'twenty years later, that George Plunket's son was laid in the same tomb; and a few years later a daughter of the said George'. He added that this George was Count Plunkett's great-grandfather. O'Hart is a notoriously unreliable source, but he cannot be dismissed entirely, especially when it comes to information about nineteenth-century happenings. Of course, it is possible that these details were supplied to O'Hart by the family.

Joseph Plunkett's grandfather, Patrick Joseph Plunkett, who allegedly was born at Killeen, survived his rebel grandson. Patrick died in Dublin on 18 December 1918 at the stated age of one hundred and one (i.e. born about 1817). According to his own account in the census returns, he was eighty in 1901 and ninety in 1911 (i.e. born about 1820–1) and was born in Dublin. However, it is more probable that he was born in Co. Meath. The newspaper announcements of his marriage in May 1847 state that he was second son of the late Mr Walter Plunkett of Julianstown, Co. Meath.[105] Unfortunately, there was more than one Julianstown in Meath. The more prominent one was in Julianstown civil parish, just south of Drogheda. In Roman Catholic divisions this was part of Stamullen parish, whose surviving baptismal records date only from 1831. The other Julianstown was a townland partly in Castletown civil (and RC) parish but mainly in Nobber civil (and RC) parish. The surviving Roman Catholic records for Castletown date from 1805 and those for Nobber date from the 1750s.

There is no reference to a Plunkett in relation to either location in the relevant Tithe Applotment Books. However, the Meath Heritage Centre's database on Rootsireland.ie reveals the baptisms of four daughters of Walter and Jane Plunkett in Nobber Roman Catholic parish. These were Bridget (1814; address Kilbride), Margaret (1818; address Argil), Elizabeth (1824; address Nobber) and Catherine (1826; address Nobber). Arrigal townland adjoins Kilbride, which adjoins Julianstown.

Two newspaper notices open further avenues of research. One refers to the marriage in New York on 9 November 1851 of Kate, youngest daughter of the late Walter Plunkett, Esq., of Julianstown, Co. Meath, to William Boyle.[106] The other relates to the death in Manchester in 1848 of George D.

Plunkett, son of the late Mr Walter Plunkett of Julianstown, Co. Meath.[107] George Daly Plunkett died on 16 August 1848 in his thirtieth year, according to his gravestone in St Chad's on Cheetham Hill Road, Manchester. An image of the gravestone and a transcript of the inscription appear online on Historicgraves.com.[108]

Kate, the youngest daughter of Walter Plunkett of Julianstown, may well have been the Catherine, daughter of Walter and Jane Plunkett, baptised in 1826. However, Catherine was one of four identified daughters of Walter and Jane Plunkett of locations other than Julianstown in Nobber parish. No sons were among the identified baptisms, but there were significant gaps in time between the first three daughters. There is a possibility that the sons were baptised in the Church of Ireland, if the parents were of mixed religions. Unfortunately, it appears that the baptismal records of Nobber C. of I. parish do not survive for the relevant period.

Another possible brother of Patrick Joseph Plunkett was identified. On 5 January 1863 in Rathmines Roman Catholic parish, Dublin, Walter Plunkett of Harold's Cross married Mary Josephine Mulloy. The register entry was in Latin and his parents were stated as 'Walteri [Plunkett] et Joannae Daly olim de Co. Meath', which translates as Walter Plunkett and Joanna/Jane Daly formerly of Co. Meath. This possible brother of Patrick Joseph would appear to be the Walter Plunkett of 26 Lower Gloucester Street, Dublin, commercial traveller, who died on 19 December 1886. Probate of his will was granted to his widow Mary Josephine.[109] This Walter's stated age at death was forty-six (born about 1820).

A Laurence Daly was sponsor to two of the daughters of Walter and Jane Plunkett in Nobber, Margaret in 1818 and Elizabeth in 1824. The Meath Heritage Centre's database on Rootsireland.ie uncovered the marriage on 28 October 1813 in Kilskyre Roman Catholic parish of Walter Plunkett and Jane Daly. Geraldine Plunkett had family memories of the O'Dalys of O'Daly's Bridge, Virginia. The bridge itself features on the National Inventory of Architectural Heritage, which shows that it is in Edenburt townland, Co. Cavan.[110] In fact the bridge straddles the border between Cos. Cavan and Meath. On the other side it is in Pottlereagh townland, Co. Meath, which a century ago contained Virginia Road railway station. This may have led Geraldine Plunkett to think O'Daly's Bridge was nearer to Virginia, which is some miles away. The Ordnance Survey 6 Inch Map (*c.*1840) shows 'Daly's Bridge' with a corn mill adjacent to it in Pottlereagh. The 25 Inch Map from the 1890s/1900s shows 'O'Daly's Bridge House' on the site of the corn mill.

Pottlereagh townland is in Kilskeer civil parish and Kilskyre Roman Catholic parish, where Walter Plunkett married Jane Daly in 1813. In Griffith's *Valuation*, John Daly had an extensive property, including a corn mill, in Pottlereagh. As revealed by the Meath Heritage Centre's database on Rootsireland.ie, John Daly and Caroline Ingram had six children baptised in Kilskyre RC parish. The online parish registers confirm that these included Louisa Bidilia in 1858 and Jemima Skyria Michel in 1863. The 1911 Census reveals that Louisa B. O'Daly was living in Pottlereagh with her widowed sister-in-law, Guadalupe O'Daly, who was born in Mexico. Geraldine Plunkett's reminiscences help to draw the Plunketts and (O)Dalys together and explain the presence of the Mexican-born family member.

It is very probable that Patrick Joseph Plunkett (born about 1817–21) and George Daly Plunkett (born about 1818–9) were sons of Walter and Jane Plunkett of Nobber parish, and that Jane was a Daly of Pottlereagh. It would appear that Walter Plunkett was a man of some status but that he became impoverished or his family did so after his death. The 'of Julianstown' may have referred back to a property no longer in the family by the 1820s. Nobber is a considerable distance north of Killeen Castle. Perhaps Lord Fingall provided Walter or his children with a farm at Killeen sometime after the birth of Catherine in 1826.

As already mentioned, there is scope for further research on Patrick Joseph Plunkett's background. The following is the *probable* structure of his immediate family.

Walter Plunkett of Julianstown, Nobber, Co. Meath (deceased by May 1847), married on 28 October 1813 in Kilskyre Roman Catholic parish Jane Daly, most likely from O'Daly's Bridge, Pottlereagh townland, and had at least seven children:

1. Bridget Plunkett; baptised in Nobber Roman Catholic parish, 22 September 1814, with address Kilbride.
2. Margaret Plunkett; baptised in Nobber, 22 March 1818, with address Argil.

3. George Daly Plunkett; born about 1818–19; died 16 August 1848 in Manchester.
4. Patrick Joseph Plunkett; born about 1817–21; died 1918; grandfather of Joseph Mary Plunkett (see below).
5. Walter Plunkett; of Harold's Cross and later 26 Lower Gloucester Street, Dublin, commercial traveller; born about 1820; married 5 January 1863 in Rathmines, Dublin, Mary Josephine Mulloy; and died 19 December 1886 in Dublin.
6. Elizabeth Plunkett; baptised in Nobber, 12 May 1824, with address Nobber.
7. Catherine (Kate) Plunkett; baptised in Nobber, 26 June 1826, with address Nobber; married 9 November 1851 at the Church of the Nativity, New York, William Boyle, late of Dublin.

Patrick Joseph Plunkett and Elizabeth Noble

Patrick Joseph Plunkett went to Dublin and prospered. It would appear that this was partly due to his marriage to Elizabeth Noble. They married in 1847 and they lived in her property in Aungier Street. According to *All in the Blood*, Plunkett acquired plots of land in Rathmines where he built new developments, while he and his wife were associated with Elizabeth's cousin Maria and her husband Patrick Cranny, another developer.

The newspaper announcements of the marriage of Patrick and Elizabeth state that she was the only surviving daughter of the late Mr John Noble of Dublin and that the marriage took place in Aungier Street, being performed by Rev. Mr Mulhall of St Andrew's, Westland Row.[111] On 16 May 1847 the register of St Andrew's Roman Catholic parish records the marriage of 'Patrick Joseph Plunket & Eliza Murphy'. This would be unrecognisable as the marriage of the same couple were it not for the family tradition preserved by Geraldine Plunkett. In *All in the Blood* she states that Elizabeth was the daughter of John Noble and Abigail O'Sullivan and that, unknown to John, Abigail arranged Elizabeth's marriage to a man named Murphy. When John found out he brought Elizabeth home and 'effectively dissolved the marriage'. Mr Murphy subsequently died, leaving everything to Elizabeth, enabling her to buy her property on the corner of Aungier Street and Stephen Street.

Patrick and Elizabeth moved their home from Aungier Street in their prosperity. They were living at 3 Belgrave Road, Rathmines, when their daughter died in 1863, and by the 1870s their residence was just around the corner at 14 Palmerston Road. This was to remain a family home until well into the twentieth century.

Patrick and Elizabeth Plunkett had four children:

1. John Plunkett; baptised in St Andrew's Roman Catholic parish, 9 April 1848, with Walter Plunkett and Maria Cranny as sponsors; died 9 April 1857 aged nine and buried in Glasnevin.[112]
2. Mary Jane Plunkett; baptised in St Andrew's, 9 December 1849, with Patrick Cranny as a sponsor;

died 20 February 1863 aged thirteen and buried in Glasnevin.[113]

3. George Noble Plunkett; baptised in St Andrew's, 7 December 1851; father of Joseph Mary Plunkett (see below).

4. Walter Daniel Plunkett; baptised in Rathmines Roman Catholic parish, 21 September 1856; died 20 March 1858 aged one and one-half and buried in the family plot in Glasnevin.

Elizabeth Plunkett died on 17 December 1873 at the stated age of sixty-four and was buried with her daughter Mary and in the plot next to her two sons. In 1877 Patrick Joseph Plunkett remarried. His new bride was Helena Mary O'Sullivan. According to Geraldine Plunkett she was another relative of Elizabeth's. They married in London, though Helena was from Dublin.[114] Patrick Plunkett had a further five children by Helena O'Sullivan:[115]

1. Germaine Margaret J. Plunkett; baptised in Rathmines Roman Catholic parish, 9 July 1878; married 12 May 1909 William John McCormack, medical doctor, of Wicklow town.

2. Angelo Plunkett; born 1 February 1881; died the following day and buried in the family plot in Glasnevin.

3. Oliver Patrick Plunkett; born 1884.

4. Helena Mary Josephine Plunkett; born 1886; married 15 July 1908 Arthur P. Barry, medical doctor, of Dublin.

5. Gerald Plunkett; born 1888; Sub-Lieutenant in the Royal Naval Volunteer Reserve; died at Gallipoli in the Great War, 4 June 1915.[116]

Patrick Joseph Plunkett died two years after his grandson Joseph, on 21 September 1918. His widow Helena died on 24 July 1933. Both were buried in the family plot in Glasnevin.

George Noble Plunkett and Mary Josephine Cranny

George Noble Plunkett was already a papal count when he married Josephine Cranny on 26 June 1884 in Donnybrook parish, Dublin. Josephine's parents were Patrick Cranny and Maria Keane, and their home at the time was Muckross Park in Marlborough Road, Donnybrook. As the church record of the marriage indicates, George and Josephine were related in the third and third degrees of consanguinity, meaning that they were second cousins.[117] Count and Countess Plunkett's children are well documented. They had seven children:

1. Philomena (Mimi) Plunkett; 1886–1926; married 12 August 1918 Jeremiah (Diarmuid) O'Leary.
2. Joseph Mary Plunkett; born 21 November 1887; married 3 May 1916 Grace Gifford.
3. Mary Josephine (Moya) Plunkett; 1889–1928.
4. Geraldine Plunkett; 1891–1986; married 23 April 1916 Thomas Dillon; she had five children, Moya (1917), Blanaid (1918), Eilís (1920), Michael (1922)

and Eoin (1929). Blanaid was the mother of the family historian Honor O Brolchain. Eilís was a well-known author.

5. George Oliver Plunkett; 1894–1944; was in the GPO during the Easter Rising with his brothers Joseph and Jack; married Mary McCarthy; his son Joseph became Count Plunkett on the death of his grandfather in 1948.
6. Josephine Mary (Fiona) Plunkett; 1896–1976.
7. John (Jack) Plunkett; 1897–1960; was in the GPO during the Easter Rising with his brothers Joseph and George.

Plunkett's Paternal Grandmother

As mentioned above, Joseph Plunkett's paternal grandmother, Elizabeth Noble, had been married (supposedly with the connivance of her mother Abigail O'Sullivan) to a Mr Murphy prior to her marriage in 1847 to Patrick Plunkett. The fact that her 1847 marriage notices referred to her as the only surviving daughter of the late Mr John Noble of Dublin and made no reference to her being a widow suggests that her first marriage was indeed 'effectively dissolved' by her father. The fact that the church record of the 1847 marriage named her as Eliza Murphy confirms that her marriage to Murphy was legal in the eyes of the Church.

If Elizabeth was a minor (under twenty-one years old) when she married Murphy without her father's consent, it would be understandable that John Noble could have the union 'effectively dissolved'. According to her stated age at death, Elizabeth was born about 1809. Therefore, she was a minor until about 1830. Edward Murphy married Elizabeth Noble in St Mary's (Pro Cathedral) parish on 5 April 1826. The witnesses were Abigail Noble and Catherine FitzGerald. Noble is an uncommon surname. The presence of Abigail Noble very strongly suggests that this is indeed the first marriage of Joseph Plunkett's grandmother. In 1826 Elizabeth Noble was about seventeen years old. It was a full twenty-one years before her marriage to Patrick Plunkett.

Elizabeth's father John Noble of Mary's Abbey died on 1 January 1840, at the stated age of sixty, and was buried in Glasnevin.[118] Her mother Abigail died a few months later, on 9 May 1840, and was buried with her husband. Her address on the burial record was Stephen Street so presumably she was living with Elizabeth at the time. Her stated age was fifty-six, so she was born about 1784. The Church Records database for Dublin on Irishgenealogy. ie reveals the baptism of only one child of John and Abigail Noble. This was recorded in Latin in the register of St Michan's Roman Catholic parish. It showed that James son of John Noble and Abigail Sullivan was baptised on 2 August 1819.

Plunkett's Maternal Grandparents

According to *All in the Blood*, Countess Plunkett's parents, Patrick Cranny and Maria Keane, met in Tralee, Co. Kerry, when Patrick went to work there. Patrick is stated as being from Borris, Co. Carlow. He worked as a shoemaker, in which trade he prospered after moving to Dublin. Later he got involved in property development. Geraldine Plunkett stated that Maria Keane's parents were 'Black John' Keane and Elizabeth O'Sullivan, and that her grandparents were Dan and Abigail O'Sullivan of Tralee, who had twenty-one children. According to their marriage record, George Noble Plunkett and Josephine Cranny were second cousins. Therefore, George's grandmother Abigail Noble née Sullivan must have been one of the twenty-one children, while Maria Keane's mother Elizabeth was another.

Patrick Cranny married Maria Keane on 26 November 1843 in St Andrew's Roman Catholic parish, Dublin, and Elizabeth Noble was one of the witnesses. In newspaper announcements of the event Patrick Cranny was described as of George's Street and Maria Keane as the eldest daughter of Mr James Keane of Tralee, cabinet maker.[119] As both announcements were from Kerry newspapers, they call into question the family tradition that Maria's father was 'Black John'. The Church Records database on Irishgenealogy.ie refers to the marriage of James Kean[e] and Elizabeth Sullivan in Tralee Roman Catholic parish on 15 June 1819 and to the baptisms of four children of parents of these names in the same parish, those of Mary in 1820, Edward in 1821, John in 1825 and Bridget in 1839. According to Maria Cranny's stated age at death she was born about 1824. Patrick and Maria Cranny had ten children:

1. John Joseph Cranny; baptised in SS Michael & John's Roman Catholic parish, 12 September 1844;

   medical doctor; married 1874 Margaret Mary Ellen
   Flanagan; died 1904.

2. Edward Cranny; baptised in SS Michael & John's,
   December 1847.

3. Mary Eliza Cranny; baptised in SS Michael &
   John's, 8 May 1849.

4. Francis Patrick Cranny; baptised in Rathmines
   Roman Catholic parish, 8 September 1850, with
   Elizabeth Plunkett as a sponsor.

5. Gerald Patrick Cranny; born about 1852.

6. Paul Daniel Cranny; baptised in Donnybrook
   Roman Catholic parish, 1854.

7. Frederick Cranny; baptised in Donnybrook, 1856.

8. Mary Josephine Cranny; baptised in Donnybrook,
   1858; mother of Joseph Mary Plunkett (see above).

9. Alfred Vincent Cranny; baptised in Donnybrook,
   1859.

10. Theobald Cranny; baptised in Donnybrook, 1860.

Patrick Cranny, Countess Plunkett's father, is said to have
been from Borris, Co. Carlow. He died in 1888, with his
stated age suggesting a birth date of 1821. The surviving
records of Borris Roman Catholic parish have a gap in the
baptisms between 1813 and 1825. There appears to be no
possibility of tracing Patrick's origins under the circumstances.
The Plunketts, Nobles and Keanes could be explored further.

ENDNOTES

1   NLI Ms. 41,479/8/15: Notes taken by Michael Kent from his father James Kent regarding his family history; http://catalogue.nli.ie/Record/vtls000585796.

2   Mary Gallagher, *16 Lives Éamonn Ceannt* (Dublin, 2014), Notes, Chapter One, No. 4; NLI ms. 41, 479/8/2: http://catalogue.nli.ie/Record/vtls000585632.

3   GRO ref.: Kilmallock, 1870/15/203.

4   Registered Number 27415.

5   Glasnevin Cemetery, St Bridget's Section, EH 118 (www.glasnevintrust.ie).

6   www.census.nationalarchive.ie/pages/1901/Dublin/Clontarf_West/Fairview_Avenue/1271130.

7   www.census.nationalarchive.ie/pages/1911/Dublin/Drumcondra/St_Alphonsus_Road/25549.

8   www.willcalendars.nationalarchives.ie/search/cwa/details.jsp?id=1639318034.

9   http://www.cwgc.org/find-war-dead/casualty/1575277/KENT,%20WILLIAM%20LEEMAN.

10 Registered Number 54068.

11 Elizabeth Thomson, 'Stratford-on-Slaney – its connection to 1916 Easter Rising', *Baltinglass Review* 2015, p. 75.

12 GRO ref.: Dublin South, 1905/Sept/2/665.

13 www.census.nationalarchives.ie/pages/1911/Dublin/New_Kilmainham/Herberton_Lane/58017.

14 www.willcalendars.nationalarchives.ie/search/cwa/details.jsp?id=1639409031.

15 GRO ref.: Dublin South, 1874/7/634; churchrecords.irishgenealogy.

ie/churchrecords/details/977aef0445403.

16   www.census.nationalarchives.ie/pages/1901/Dublin/Ushers_
     Quay/South_Dublin_Union/1303078.

17   http://mspcsearch.militaryarchives.ie/brief.aspx.

18   Louis N. Le Roux, *Tom Clarke and the Irish Freedom Movement*
     (Dublin, 1936), p. 7.

19   Tom Clarke and Kathleen Clarke Papers, National Library of
     Ireland Ms. 49,355/8.

20   GRO ref.: Clogheen, 1857/3/630.

21   www.findmypast.com, British Army Service Records 1760-1915:
     James Clarke, born 1830, event 1847, location Carrigallin, Leitrim,
     Ireland.

22   www.rootsireland.ie, Leitrim Genealogy Centre database.

23   National Library of Ireland, Pos. 4646.

24   GRO ref.: Clogheen, 1883/June/4/472.

25   GRO ref.: Clogheen, 1883/Sept./4/354.

26   Le Roux, *Tom Clarke*, p. 8.

27   Tom Clarke and Kathleen Clarke Papers, National Library of
     Ireland Ms. 49,351/4/18, Letter from Tom Clarke to Kathleen
     Clarke, 19 September 1905.

28   Helen Litton, *Thomas Clarke* (Dublin, 2014), p. 225.

29   Ibid., p. 224.

30   Ibid., p. 18.

31   www.rootsireland.ie, Limerick Genealogy database; he was actually
     42.

32   Ibid.

33   www.scotlandspeople.gov.uk; *The Catholic Directory for the Year*,
     1856.

34   'R.E. Matheson's Special Report on Surnames in Ireland', reproduced
     in Donal F. Begley (ed.), *Irish Genealogy: A Record Finder* (Dublin,
     1981).

35   Lorcan Collins, *16 Lives James Connolly* (Dublin, 2012), p. 34.

36   Ibid., pp. 33, 74.

37   Ibid., pp. 42, 127, 131.

38   Ibid., p. 42.

39   GRO ref.: Manorhamilton, 1874/12/155.

40   GRO ref.: Manorhamilton, 1895/March/2/192.

41   http://censussearchforms.nationalarchives.ie/search/cs/details.
      jsp?id=36302.

42   GRO ref.: Manorhamilton, 1904/June/2/173.

43   GRO ref.: Manorhamilton, 1904/March/2/190.

44   GRO ref.: Manorhamilton, 1892/March/2/218.

45   GRO ref.: Manorhamilton, 1913/Dec/2/139.

46   www.ancestry.com, New York, Passenger Lists, 1820-1957.

47   James McGuire & James Quinn (eds), *Dictionary of Irish Biography:
      from the earliest times to the year 2002* (Cambridge, 2009), entry for
      Seán Mac Diarmada.

48   www.ancestry.com, New York, Passenger Lists, 1820-1957.

49   http://mspcsearch.militaryarchives.ie/brief.aspx.

50   GRO ref.: Borrisokane, 1894/March/3/324.

51   www.forgottenbooks.com.

52   NLI Ms. 44,324/1: Letter from John Rochford to Mary MacDonagh
      ... (in the NLI online catalogue she is mistakenly identified as Sister
      Francesca).

53   Smyrl, Steven C., *Dictionary of Dublin Dissent: Dublin's Protestant
      Dissenting Meeting Houses 1660-1920* (Dublin, 2009), pp. 39-53.

54   www.thegazette.co.uk/London/issue/23441/page/5887/data.pdf.

55   www.ancestry.co.uk, London, England, Electoral Registers, 1832-
      1965 (source: London Metropolitan Archives).

56   www.ancestry.co.uk, London, England, Marriages and Banns, 1754-
      1921 (source: London Metropolitan Archives).

57   www.ancestry.co.uk, London, England, Freedom of the City
      Admission Papers, 1681-1925 (source: London Metropolitan
      Archives); www.spectaclemakers.com/company/history.html.

58   GRO England & Wales ref.: Islington, 1840/Sept/3/185.

59   GRO England & Wales ref.: Islington, 1842/Sept/3/226.

60   http://mspcsearch.militaryarchives.ie/brief.aspx.

61   www.ancestry.co.uk, London, England, Births and Baptisms, 1813-
      1906 (source: London Metropolitan Archives).

62   www.familysearch.org, England Marriages, 1538-1973 (https://
      familysearch.org/ark:/61903/1:1:NJY1-24S).

63   Róisín Ní Ghairbhí, *16 Lives Willie Pearse* (Dublin, 2015), p. 26.

64   Ibid., p. 33.

65   www.ancestry.co.uk, London, England, Births and Baptisms, 1813–1906 (source: London Metropolitan Archives).

66   www.ancestry.co.uk, Birmingham, England, Marriages and Banns, 1754–1937 (source: Library of Birmingham).

67   GRO England & Wales ref: Birmingham, 1866/June/6d/135.

68   www.ancestry.co.uk, Birmingham, England, Marriages and Banns, 1754–1937 (source: Library of Birmingham).

69   www.ancestry.co.uk, London, England, Births and Baptisms, 1813–1906 (source: London Metropolitan Archives).

70   Ibid.

71   www.ancestry.co.uk, Birmingham, England, Marriages and Banns, 1754–1937 (source: Library of Birmingham).

72   Ní Ghairbhí, *Willie Pearse*, pp. 256-7; www.cwgc.org/find-war-dead/casualty/808990/PEARSE,%20HARRY.

73   www.dia.ie/architects/view/4302/PEARSE-JAMES%2A.

74   www.ancestry.co.uk, Birmingham, England, Marriages and Banns, 1754–1937 (source: Library of Birmingham).

75   Glasnevin Cemetery, Garden Section, CE 59½ (www.glasnevintrust.ie).

76   NLI Ms. 21,077: Letter from Pius Devine to James Pearse.

77   www.dia.ie/architects/view/4302/PEARSE-JAMES%2A.

78   Ní Ghairbhí, *Willie Pearse*, p. 50; www.willcalendars.nationalarchives.ie/search/cwa/details.jsp?id=1639527283.

79   Possibly part of what is now Windsor Terrace.

80   www.dia.ie/architects/view/3872/MCGLOUGHLIN-ALFREDignatius.

81   GRO ref: Milford, 1909/March/2/285.

82   http://mspcsearch.militaryarchives.ie/search.aspx.

83   Ibid.

84   Possibly a different name for Pleasant View.

85   Ní Ghairbhí, *Willie Pearse*, pp. 55 & 116-17.

86   Ibid., pp. 181 & 255.

87   Ibid., p. 292, notes 13-14.

88   Ibid., pp. 180-1 & 255.

89   GRO ref.: 1933/Dec./2/640.

90 www.census.nationalarchives.ie/pages/1911/Dublin/Rathfarnham/ Rathfarnham_Village/49201.

91 www.census.nationalarchives.ie/pages/1911/Dublin/Whitechurch/ Haroldsgrange_/57855.

92 Ní Ghairbhí, *Willie Pearse*, pp. 27-8.

93 Ibid., pp. 19 & 29-30.

94 www.ancestry.co.uk: Griffith's Valuation database; www. askaboutireland.ie: Griffith's Valuation database.

95 Glasnevin Cemetery, Garden Section, YF 211 (www.glasnevintrust.ie).

96 www.irishnewsarchive.com: *Cork Examiner*, 12 January 1871.

97 Glasnevin Cemetery, Garden Section, ZF 211½ (www.glasnevintrust. ie).

98 www.willcalendars.nationalarchives.ie/search/cwa/details.jsp?id= 1639501688.

99 Ní Ghairbhí, *Willie Pearse*, pp. 33 & 57-8.

100 Ibid., p. 257; www.telegraph.co.uk/news/obituaries/9174638/Patrick-Shovelton.html.

101 Ní Ghairbhí, *Willie Pearse*, p. 58.

102 Among the assorted Pearse family certificates in NLI Ms. 21,077 is a letter dated 21.11.08 from the Parish Priest of Rochfortbridge certifying the baptism on 24 November 1829 of Jane Fox, daughter of John Fox and Eliza Cole.

103 Her birth certificate is among the assorted Pearse family certificates in NLI Ms. 21,077. Incidentally her baptismal record states that she was born on 4 January and baptised on 8 January.

104 Dillon, Geraldine Plunkett (ed. Honor O Brolchain), *All in the Blood: A Memoir of the Plunkett Family, the 1916 Rising and the War of Independence* (Dublin, 2006).

105 www.irishnewsarchive.com: *Freeman's Journal*, 20 May 1847, *The Leinster Express*, 22 May 1847.

106 www.findmypast.com, Irish Newspapers: *Catholic Telegraph*, 17 January 1852.

107 www.findmypast.com, Irish Newspapers: *The Pilot*, 21 August 1848.

108 www.historicgraves.com/st-chad-s/gm-stcd-0005/grave.

109 www.willcalendars.nationalarchives.ie/search/cwa/details.jsp?id= 1639533736.

110 www.buildingsofireland.ie/niah/search.jsp?type=record&county=C
     V&regno=40404402.
111 www.irishnewsarchive.com: *Freeman's Journal*, 20 May 1847, *The
     Leinster Express*, 22 May 1847.
112 Glasnevin Cemetery, Garden Section, TC 59 (www.glasnevintrust.ie).
113 Glasnevin Cemetery, Garden Section, TC 59½ (www.glasnevintrust.ie).
114 GRO England & Wales ref: London City, 1877/Sept./1c/153.
115 According to the 1911 Census Helena had five children, of whom
     four were then living.
116 http://www.cwgc.org/find-war-dead/casualty/3054942/
     PLUNKETT,%20GERALD.
117 http://churchrecords.irishgenealogy.ie/churchrecords/details/
     fff4e30041028.
118 Glasnevin Cemetery, Garden Section, YC 36 (www.glasnevintrust.ie).
119 www.irishnewsarchive.com: *Kerry Examiner*, 1 December 1843,
     Tralee Chronicle and Killarney Echo, 2 December 1843.